Privacy and Data Protection Law in Brazil

Privacy and Data Protection Law in Brazil

Patricia Peck Pinheiro

This book was originally published as a monograph in the International Encyclopaedia of Laws/Privacy and Technology Law.

Founding Editor: Roger Blanpain
General Editor: Frank Hendrickx
Volume Editors: Jos Dumortier, Pieter Gryffroy, Ruben Roex &
Yung Shin Van Der Sype

Wolters Kluwer

Published by:
Kluwer Law International B.V.
PO Box 316
2400 AH Alphen aan den Rijn
The Netherlands
E-mail: lrs-sales@wolterskluwer.com
Website: www.wolterskluwer.com/en/solutions/kluwerlawinternational

Sold and distributed by:
Wolters Kluwer Legal & Regulatory U.S.
920 Links Avenue
Landisville, PA 17538
United States of America
E-mail: customer.service@wolterskluwer.com

ISBN 978-94-035-3526-5

e-Book: ISBN 978-94-035-4006-1
web-PDF: ISBN 978-94-035-4016-0

The Author

Patricia Peck Pinheiro, born in 1975 in Rio de Janeiro, Brazil, studied high school in Rio de Janeiro and graduated from the Law School of São Paulo University (USP) in 1998. She has more than twenty years of experience working with Cyber Law and Technology Innovation in Brazil and is the author and co-author of forty books on Digital Law Practice. She is a strong entrepreneurship professional and the founder of Peck Law Firm, with more than one hundred professionals. Patricia is skilled in Privacy and Data Protection, Cyber Security, Arbitration, IP and Comparative Law of Brazil, Latin America, Europe, and the United States of America, with a Doctor of Philosophy (Ph.D.) focused on International Law and Intellectual Property Law which she has received from USP. She is a Council Member of the Brazil Data Protection Authority. She is Law Professor at ESPM University. She has been an international researcher at the Max Planck Institute in Hamburg and Munich and at Columbia University. In addition, she has been an invited Guest Speaker at Coimbra University Law School in Portugal, with lectures on the topic of Digital Contracts and Brazilian Data Protection Regulation (Comparative Law).

The author thanks the following people for their valuable contributions:

Bruna Kruger
Bruna Godoy
Camila Nascimento
Gabriel Toscano
Julia Ramos
Larissa Lotufo
Lucas Arthuso
Lucas Galdino
Matheus Rocha
Mellany Prawda
Milena Grado
Roberta Teofilo

The Author

Table of Contents

List of Abbreviations

ABNT	Brazilian Technical Standards Association
ABRAJI	Brazilian Association of Investigative Journalism
AEPD	Agencia Española de Protección de Datos
ANPD	Brazilian Data Protection Authority
BCRs	Binding Corporate Rules
CDC	Consumer's Rights Act
CJEU	Court of Justice of the European Union
CJF	Federal Court Council
CNJ	Brazilian Councils of Justice
CNMP	Public Prosecutor's Office
CNS	Brazilian National Council of Health
CPF	Cadastro de Pessoa Física
DPA	Data Protection Authority
DPIAs	Data Protection Impact Assessments
DPO	Data Protection Officer
EDPB	European Data Protection Board
EDPS	European Data Protection Supervisor
EIRELI	Limited Liability Sole Proprietorship
EU	European Union
DGP	Personnel Management Board
DTI	Information Technology Directorate
GDPR	General Data Protection Regulation
IAPP	International Association of Privacy Professionals
IBGE	Brazilian Institute of Geography and Statistics
ICO	Information Commissioner's Office
ICT	Information and Communication Technology
IEC	International Electrotechnical Commission
ISO	International Organization for Standardization
LED	Law Enforcement Directive (EU) 2016/680
LGPD	Brazilian Data Protection Law

List of Abbreviations

MLATs	Mutual Legal Assistance Treaties
MPF	General Public Attorney's Office
OAB	Brazilian Bar Association
OAS	Organization of American States
OECD	Organisation for Economic Co-operation and Development
PEC	Constitution Amendment Proposal
RIPD	Red Iberoamericana de Protección de Datos
SARS	Severe Acute Respiratory Syndrome
SCCs	Standard Contractual Clauses
SENACOM	National Secretariat of Consumers
STF	Supreme Federal Court
STJ	Superior Court of Justice
TCU	Federal Court of Accounts
UWG	German Law Against Unfair Competition
WAF	Web Application Firewall
WEF	World Economic Forum
WP29	Working Party 29

General Introduction

1. Since August 14, 2018, Brazil has had a general Law for the Protection of Personal Data, the Brazilian Data Protection Law, known as LGPD (Law 13.709/2018). Inspired by the European Regulation n. 2016/679, the national regulation came into force in September 2020 and has had the possibility of applying fines since August 2021. Brazil already has its own National Data Protection Authority (ANPD) in place, but there are still many challenges for Brazil to reach a higher stage of data protection culture, and this is most likely due to the specific characteristics of the country, its complexity and size.

2. It is also important to observe that Brazilian Law No. 13,709/2018 (LGPD) has already been amended several times so far:

- Provisional Measure No. 869 of December 2018, edited by President Michel Temer, which was later converted into Law No. 13.853/19, promoted some changes in the text, created ANPD and included the extension of the period of adaptation and adequacy until August 2020 (initially scheduled for February).
- Provisional Measure No. 959, of April 29, 2020, edited by President Jair Bolsonaro, determined the entry into force of the LGPD in its entirety, including sanctions, for May 3, 2021.
- then, on June 10, 2020, the head of the Executive Branch partially sanctioned Bill 1,179/20, which dealt, among other matters, with the postponement of the application of sanctions related to the General Data Protection Law to August 1, 2021—this act, which was instituted to transitory and emergency rules for the regulation of legal relations under Private Law due to the coronavirus pandemic (COVID-19), gave rise to Law No. 14,010 of 2020.

3. The delay of the data protection agenda in Brazil is much related to difficulties in adapting to the LGPD caused by the strong impact that the COVID-19 pandemic has been causing during the same period on all economic sectors, either public or private, but especially to the small and medium enterprises and start-ups. Another reason was the late establishment of the ANPD. Besides, it is inevitable to acknowledge that all this delay caused the awareness of privacy and data protection to increase and spread not only among companies but to people themselves, who are employees or citizens using services, and the absence of knowledge on this matter causes a gap which is used, so the consequences of this are that the last year of 2021 was marked by huge data leaks that brought irreversible damage to Brazilian citizens, caused by lack of security measures and culture on cyber security.

4. In a sense, the Brazilian Government might have underestimated the time needed to implement this kind of regulation, which demands financial investments and the support of public policies providing incentives to comply with the law, which were not provided at their best. In addition, there is a lack of education on cyber security culture and a lack of best practices to help build a more sustainable environment for Data Protection.

5. As a consequence of these circumstances mentioned before, at the same time Brazil is trying to have its most compliance with the national data protection law, it is facing one of the highest rates of cyberattacks. LGPD case law is slowly emerging, showing that the judicialization of the matter is inevitable by people suing companies where they might find the smallest sign of their data being processed. Besides, it is important to ensure that the ANPD leads the way in interpreting the law to avoid legal uncertainty, which may be caused by the lack of expertise faced by some of the local courts around the country; It is quite necessary to keep in mind that Brazil is a country of continental proportion, with many local justice courts, and that the data protection theme is quite recent.

6. For the near future, the expectation is that the ANPD will start the monitoring cycle of inspection, and that will contribute to the enforcement of the Law. Besides, there will be new updates on the regulation regarding priority topics, such as international data transfer, data subject rights, cybersecurity requirements, Data Protection Officer (DPO) activities and anonymization.

Part I. Privacy Protection in Brazil

Chapter 1. Privacy Protection in the Constitution

7. The right to privacy is contained in Article 5 of the Brazilian Constitution of 1988. It is considered a fundamental right—the development of data protection rights.

8. Privacy and Data Protection are two different but correlated notions that many times confuse themselves into one.

9. In 1890, The Right to Privacy[1] was published in the Harvard Law Review journal, and it is considered a landmark as the first publication in the United States to advocate the right to privacy. It is commonly known for defining privacy as the right to be left alone.

10. In this monograph, the authors questioned if there would be, in common law, a fundament to guarantee individuals' protection of privacy and what would be its nature and extension.

11. The content of the article exposes situations where the breach of a contract and, consequently, the confidence were used to solve many cases; however, the violation of private life won't always be attributable to a contractor. It was also mentioned that the right to property to protect immaterial goods, as it was, would not be enough in a modern world.

12. The article ends by indicating that the protection of privacy rests on the right to privacy, which its affected by the broader right of personality.

13. Afterward, the right to privacy was coded on an international level composing the Universal Declaration of Human Rights, drafted in 1948, right after the Second World War, even before it was included in any bill of rights.

1. Samuel D. Warren & Louis D. Brandeis, *The Right to Privacy*, 4(5) Harv. L. Rev.w 193–220 (1890). *JSTOR*. Available at: www.jstor.org/stable/1321160. Access on: Nov. 17, 2021.

14. In Article 12, the Declaration stipulates:

> No one shall be subjected to arbitrary interference with his privacy, family, home or correspondence, nor to attacks upon his honor and reputation. Everyone has the right to the protection of the law against such interference or attacks.[2]

15. There are at least two core ideas that compete on what privacy is about, according to Diggelmann and Cleis,[3] which are privacy as freedom from society and privacy as dignity.

16. With the advent of modern computing, a new concept was born: informational privacy, which today we call data protection. This granted individuals to have some sort of control over their information.

17. A main change that affected the right to privacy was the recognition of the individual, and not its property, as the object of protection by this right.[4]

18. During the subsequent years, many legislations, regulations, and directives were designed to protect individuals' right to privacy and data protection, and in some countries, including Brazil, it even became part of Constitutions as a fundamental right.

19. In 1980, the Organisation for Economic Co-operation and Development (OECD) adopted the Guidelines on the Protection of Privacy and Transborder Flows of Personal Data, aiming to contribute to a global free flow of personal data.

20. The set of common principles that rise from such new documents contributed to the edition of privacy definitions and regulations as we see them today.

21. In Europe, the first ruling happened at Directive 95/46/EC of the European Parliament and of the Council of October 24, 1995, on the protection of individuals regarding the processing of personal data and on the free movement of such data.

22. However, over the years, the Directive became outdated, and the necessity of a new form of legislation emerged.

23. The European Commission 2012 presented new objectives they wanted to achieve with the elaboration of a new legislation, which was full harmonization into one unified regulation, improvement of user control and the improvement of corporate data transfer rules outside the EU.

---

2. UN General Assembly, *Universal Declaration of Human Rights*, Dec. 10, 1948, 217 A (III). Available at: https://www.refworld.org/docid/3ae6b3712c.html. Access on: Nov, 17, 2021.
3. Oliver Diggelmann & Maria Nicole Cleis, *How the Right to Privacy Became a Human Right*, 14(3) Human Rights L. Rev. 441–458 (September 2014). Available at: https://doi.org/10.1093/hrlr/ngu014. Access on: Nov. 17, 2021.
4. Danilo Doneda, *Da privacidade à proteção de dados pessoais* 284 (Renovar 2006).

24. Finally, the Regulation (EU) 2016/679 of the European Parliament and of the Council, on April 27, 2016, on the protection of natural persons with regard to the processing of personal data and the free movement of such data was published, establishing the so-called General Data Protection Regulation[5] (GDPR) which repealed Directive 95/46/EC.

25. In Brazil, the first-time personal data protection was legally mentioned was in 2014, in Law 12.965 (Brazilian Internet Law Framework—Marco Civil da Internet). Data protection was then considered a principle related to the use of the Internet, and it was established in its second article:[6]

> Article 2. Regulation of the Internet in Brazil shall be grounded on the recognition of the international nature of the Internet, the exercise of citizenship in the digital environment, human rights, the values of plurality, diversity, openness and collaboration, free enterprise and free competition, considering the following principles:
> II—protection of privacy; III—protection of personal data, in accordance to the law;"

26. However, the right to privacy has appeared on the legal framework since the development of the new Federal Constitution (1988), which included the right in Article 5, X[7] as a fundamental right:

> Article 5. All persons are equal before the law, without any distinction whatsoever, Brazilians and foreigners residing in the country being ensured of inviolability of the right to life, to liberty, to equality, to security and to property, on the following terms: […]
> X—the privacy, private life, honor and image of persons are inviolable, and the right to compensation for property or moral damages resulting from their violation is ensured;

27. The right to privacy is also included in the Habeas Data law, Public Files Law, Brazilian Civil Code, Consumer Protection Code, Access to Information Law, and then, most recently, on the Brazilian Internet Law Framework, as mentioned above.

28. For years, a specific legislation on data protection was much craved by legal professionals. Certainly, the pressure imposed by privacy scandals, such as the

5. Regulation (EU) 2016/679 of the European Parliament and of the Council of 27 April 2016 on the protection of natural persons with regard to the processing of personal data and on the free movement of such data and repealing Directive 95/46/EC (General Data Protection Regulation), OJ 2016 L 119/1.
6. Brasil, Lei No. 12.965, Marco Civil da Internet, 2014. Available at: http://www.planalto.gov.br/ccivil_03/_ato2011-2014/2014/lei/l12965.htm. Access on: Nov. 20, 2021.
7. Brasil, Constituição da República Federativa do Brasil de 1988. Available at: http://planalto.gov.br/ccivil_03/constituicao/constituicao.htm. Access on: Nov. 20, 2021.

Cambridge Analytica,[8] and the international commitments, especially the GDPR, which requires an essentially adequate level of protection for the free flow of data with third countries, were fundamental for the development of the Brazilian General Data Protection Law (hereinafter referred to as "LGPD").

29. Nowadays, 126 countries have a specific legislation on personal data protection; however, in South America, only Argentina and Uruguay have compatible regulations with the GDPR.[9]

30. The approval of Law No. 13.709/18,[10] which created the LGPD, only happened on July 10, 2018, after more than 2.500 (two thousand and five hundred) public consultations, including with European Union, and its publication occurred on August 15, 2018, with partial sanctions.

31. Later, on May 29, 2019, the Provisory Measure No. 869/2018, approved by the Federal Senate, altered and added articles to the LGPD, including the creation of the ANPD, however, as a transitory organ directly related to the Presidency.

32. It should be noted that the right to privacy is in line with the fundamental principles of the Republic expressed in the Brazilian Constitution of 1988, especially respect for human dignity, the construction of a free, fair, and solidary society and the promotion of the good of all without prejudice.[11]

33. Article 1. The Federative Republic of Brazil, formed by the indissoluble union of the States and Municipalities and of the Federal District, is a legal democratic state and is founded on:

> III—the dignity of the human person;

34. Article 3. The fundamental objectives of the Federative Republic of Brazil are:

> I—to build a free, just and solidary society;
> IV—to promote the well-being of all, without prejudice as to origin, race, sex, colour, age and any other forms of discrimination.

---

8. Alvin Chang, *The Facebook and Cambridge Analytica Scandal Explained with a Simple Diagram* (Vox 2018). Available at: https://www.vox.com/policy-and-politics/2018/3/23/17151916/facebook-cambridge-analytica-trump-diagram. Accessed on: Nov. 21, 2021.
9. Leonardo Henrique de Carvalho Ventura, *Considerações sobre a nova lei geral de proteção de dados*. 13(155) Revista Síntese: Direito Administrativo 56/64 (2018).
10. Brasil, Lei Geral De Proteção De Dados Pessoais. Lei no 13.709, de 14 de agosto de 2018. Available at: http://www.planalto.gov.br/ccivil_03/_ato2015-2018/2018/lei/l13709.htm. Accessed on: Nov. 21, 2021.
11. Constitution of the Federative Republic of Brazil: constitutional text enacted on October 5, 1988, with the alterations established by Revision Constitutional Amendments No. 1, 1994 through 6, 1994, by Constitutional Amendments No. 1, 1992 through 92, 2016, and by Legislative Decree No. 186, 2008.—5th ed.—Brasília: Chamber of Deputies, Edições Câmara, 2016 (Série textos básicos; n. 132 PDF).

35. Given the characteristics of historicity and the inexhaustibility of fundamental rights, others can be built and included in the protection provided to interests endowed with legal relevance (Article 5, § 2, CF/88), especially considering the dynamics of economic and social aspects of the production/reproduction of contemporary life. It was in this context that the data appeared as legal assets protected by the legal system, which led us to its final and direct presence on the Brazilian Constitution, as it will be better addressed later on.

36. José Afonso da Silva, one of the most respectable constitutionalists in Brazil, had written the following about privacy and the Brazilian constitution many years before LGPD was enacted:[12]

> The intense development of a complex network of electronic files, especially on personal data, constitutes a powerful threat to people's privacy. The extensive computerized information system generates a scrutiny process of people, who keep their individuality fully explored. (…) The constitution has not neglected this threat.

37. Accordingly, the privacy rights subject of Article 5 of the Brazilian Constitution of 1988 encompasses data protection rights.

38. Furthermore, the same Article 5 establishes a rule that a data subject shall obtain information oneself in government data bases.

39. LXXII—habeas data shall be granted:

(a) to ensure the knowledge of information related to the person of the petitioner, contained in records or data banks of government agencies or of agencies of a public character;
(b) for the correction of data, when the petitioner does not prefer to do so through a confidential process, either judicial or administrative;

40. This rule has some limitations; however, it must be taken into consideration that it is a constitutional recognition of data protection rights.[13]

41. It should be noted that the Federal Supreme Court itself, in the recent judgment of Direct Unconstitutionality Actions 6387, 6388, 6389, 6390 and 6393, recognizes data protection as a constitutional right, as shown by the vote of the Reporting Minister Rosa Weber, followed by the overwhelming majority of the Supreme Court (10 votes to 1):

> I understand that the conditions under which the manipulation of digitized personal data occurs, by public or private agents, is one of the greatest

12. José Afonso Silva, *Curso de Direito Constitucional Positivo*, 30th edn. Malheiros Editores, 209.
13. Laura Schertel Mendes, *Privacidade, proteção de dados e defesa do consumidor* 168 (Saraiva 1st ed. 2014).

contemporary challenges of the right to privacy. The Constitution of the Republic grants special protection to the intimacy, private life, honor and image of people by qualifying them as inviolable, as fundamental rights of the personality, ensuring compensation for material or moral damage resulting from their violation (art. 5, X). The so-called right to privacy and its associated rights to intimacy, honor and image stem from the recognition that the individual personality deserves to be protected in all its manifestations. In order to implement such rights, the Constitution provides, in art. 5, XII, the inviolability of the 'secrecy of correspondence and telegraphic, data and telephone communications, except, in the latter case, by court order, in the cases and in the manner established by law for the purposes of criminal investigation or criminal prosecution'.

42. Finally, it is important to note that the Chamber of Deputies approved the Senate's Constitution Amendment Proposal (PEC) 17/19, which makes personal data protection, including in digital media, a fundamental right and refers privately to the Federal Union to legislate on the subject.

43. The proposal was approved in two rounds in the form of a substitute for the rapporteur and should return to the Senate due to the changes made.

44. According to the proposal, the Federal Union will also be responsible for organizing and supervising the protection and processing of personal data under the terms of the law.

Chapter 2. National Application of Regional and International Conventions

45. The Universal Declaration of Human Rights and the American Convention on Human Rights were the seed for privacy protection in Brazil. An important Federal Supreme Court decision about data protection mentions these two treaties.

46. It is from the Universal Declaration of Human Rights[14] that the right to privacy came to be seen as a human and fundamental right belonging to everyone.

47. Article 12. No one shall be subjected to arbitrary interference with his privacy, family, home or correspondence, nor to attacks upon his honor and reputation. Everyone has the right to the protection of the law against such interference or attacks.

48. It can be seen, therefore, that the right to privacy, property, and personal security, related to each other and undeniably connected to the logic of the necessary protection of personal data, are raised to the level of supranational rights and fundamental guarantees required by any human being, bearing in mind that they are interconnected with what has come to be called the 'principle of human dignity.

49. In the same perspective as the Universal Declaration of Human Rights, the text of the American Convention on Human Rights, established in 1969 and widely known as the "Pact of San Jose, Costa Rica," enacted in Brazil by Decree No. 678/1923, which provides in its Article 11:

(1) Everyone has the right to have his honor respected and his dignity recognized.
(2) No one may be the object of arbitrary or abusive interference with his private life, his family, his home, or his correspondence, or of unlawful attacks on his honor or reputation.
(3) Everyone has the right to the protection of the law against such interference or attacks.

50. The right to privacy, within the Brazilian normative structure, is also protected by the Civil Code, especially in its Article 21, concerning the rights related to the personality of each individual, when it addresses that "the private life of a natural person is inviolable, and the judge, at the request of the interested party, shall adopt the necessary measures to prevent or stop an act contrary to this norm."[15]

51. Besides the civil provision, the right to privacy is also broadly protected in the criminal arena, especially through the following articles: Article 151 relates to

14. UN General Assembly, *Universal Declaration of Human Rights*, Dec. 10, 1948, 217 A (III). Available at: https://www.refworld.org/docid/3ae6b3712c.html. Access on Oct. 3, 2021.
15. Brazil, Law No. 10.406, Jan. 10, 2002. Establishes the Civil Code. Official Journal of the Union: Section 1, Brasília, DF, year 139, n. 8, pp. 1–74, Jan. 11, 2002.

the crime of violation of correspondences, and Articles 153, 154 and 154-A aim to protect the citizens from crimes against the inviolability of secrets.[16]

52. It is also important to notice that the spirit of the inter-American norm received in Brazil and the other presented national regulations is the same as that expressed since 1948 in the UN norm: guaranteeing the right to privacy and secrecy as intrinsic to the condition of human beings.

53. These two provisions were pointed out in the main Brazilian court decision on the protection of personal data, a decision of the Supreme Court to declare unconstitutional the Executive Decree 954/2020 enacted by President Jair Bolsonaro that obliged private telecommunications companies to transfer to the federal government from Brazilian Institute of Geography and Statistics (IBGE), personal data of consumers, under the argument of endorsing the Severe Acute Respiratory Syndrome (SARS)-Cov-2 statistics.

54. Direct Unconstitutionality Actions were filed against this Provisional Measure by 4 political parties and by the Federal Council of the Brazilian Bar Association (OAB) [4], under the common argument that such Public Attorney's Office, by forcing fixed and mobile telephony companies to make the list of names available to the IBGE Foundation, the telephone numbers and addresses of its consumers, natural or legal persons, violates the provisions of the Constitution that ensure the dignity of the human person, the inviolability of intimacy, private life, honor and image of people and secrecy of the data.

55. The right to privacy is enshrined in international human rights treaties ratified by the Brazilian State. It is in Article 12 of the Universal Declaration of Human Rights and in Article 17 of the International Covenant on Civil and Political Rights (1966), hereby establishing: "1. No one shall be the object of arbitrary or unlawful interference with his private life, family, home or correspondence, nor of unlawful offenses to his honor and reputation. 2. Everyone shall be entitled to the protection of the law against such interference or offences." Also, Article 11 of the American Convention on Human Rights (1969) has: "1. ... 2. No one may be the object of arbitrary or abusive interference in his private life, family, home or correspondence, nor of illegal offenses to his honor or reputation. 3. Everyone is entitled to the protection of the law against such interference or such offence." In case of restriction on the right to privacy, the International Human Rights Law requires that a limit be defined only if it is to achieve a legitimate objective—for example, the protection of public health—but provided that it is necessary and proportional to the objective pursued.

56. In Brazil, Privacy has Constitutional Protection in Article 5.

---

16. Brazil, Decree-Law No. 2.848, Dec. 7, 1940. Criminal Code. Official Journal of the Union, Rio de Janeiro, Dec. 31, 1940.

57. Finally, it is important to notice that Brazilian LGPD is a recently enacted piece of legislation, and therefore there are not many decisions about it, especially in the superior courts. Decisions in lower instances are typically based on the Brazilian Constitution of 1988 and other legislation.

Chapter 3. Privacy in Electronic Communications

58. The Brazilian Civil Rights Framework for Internet is one main piece of legislation in electronic communication. There is no legislation treating specifically about cookies.

59. Before entering the electronic communication scope, it is necessary to talk about Law 9.472/1997. It organizes telecommunication services in Brazil. In its Article 3, it establishes the right to communication secrecy and privacy. Moreover, it also establishes the user's right to oppose its data disclosure. Therefore, it must be considered the beginning of what was about to come.

60. The main legislation in electronic communications is the Brazilian Civil Rights Framework for the Internet (Marco Civil da Internet, officially Law No 12.965/2014) which enacts principles, guarantees, rights and duties to those who use the Internet.

61. The law is totally related to data protection as it establishes its principles: privacy and data protection.

62. Furthermore, the Brazilian Civil Rights Framework for the Internet, in its Article 7, also establishes a myriad of rights related to privacy and data protection, for example, intimacy inviolability, impossibility of sharing data with third parties, except through previous consent, and clear and complete information about data processing.

63. Article 7.[17] Internet access is essential for the exercise of citizenship rights and duties, and users have the right to:

> I — privacy and private life, and to compensation for material and moral damages resulting from violation of the right to privacy and private life;
> II — confidentiality of communications made via the Internet, which may only be disclosed by judicial order in the manner provided for by law;
> III — confidentiality of stored private communications, which may only be disclosed by judicial order;
> IV — maintenance of Internet connection, unless it is terminated due to the user's failure to pay for its use;
> V — a consistent Internet connection in accordance with the quality contracted with the provider
> VI — clear and complete information in contracts with Internet service providers, including a detailed description of the measures taken to protect connection logs and Internet application access logs, and of network management practices that could affect the quality of the service;

17. C.A. Souza, M. Viola & R. Lemos, *Brazil's Internet Bill of Rights: A Closer Look* 11 (ITS Rio 2d ed. 2018).

VII — non-disclosure of their personal data to third parties, including connection logs and Internet application access logs, except with their free, express, and informed consent or in the cases provided for by law;

VIII — clear and comprehensive information on the collection, use, storage, and protection of users' personal data, which may only be used for purposes that:

a) justify collecting the data;
b) are not prohibited by law; and
c) are specifically stated in Internet service contracts or in terms and conditions for use of Internet applications.

IX — express consent for the collection, use, storage, and processing of personal data, which must be presented in a way that distinguishes the consent clause from the other contractual clauses

X — full removal of personal data supplied to Internet applications, at the users request, at the end of the agreement between the parties, except when this Law requires records to be kept;

XI — policies on use that are clear and publicized, when Internet service providers or Internet applications providers adopt such policies;

XII — accessibility, taking into account users' physical, motor, perceptual, sensory, intellectual, and mental abilities, as provided for by law; and

XIII — application of consumer protection rules to consumer relations that take place on the Internet.

64. Specifically taking into consideration communications, the Brazilian Civil Rights Framework for the Internet establishes that:

> Art. 10. Maintenance and disclosure of Internet connection logs and Internet application access logs contemplated in this Law, of personal data, and of the content of private communications must respect the privacy, private life, honor, and image of the parties directly or indirectly involved
> Art. 11. All operations involving the collection, storage, retention or processing of records, personal data, or communications by Internet service and applications providers must comply with Brazilian law and the rights to privacy, protection of personal data, and confidentiality of private communications and records, if any of those acts occur in Brazilian territory

65. It must be considered that the Brazilian Civil Rights Framework for the Internet does not have a provision directly related to cookies, and neither does the Brazilian LGPD (Lei Geral de Proteção de Dados). Therefore, it is possible to understand that the cookie warning is not an obligation in Brazil; however, it is being adopted as the best privacy practice.

66. Finally, it is relevant to talk about the Decree which regulates the Brazilian Civil Rights Framework for the Internet (Decree 8.771/2016). It has a specific chapter about data protection which establishes, for example, that personal data should be kept for a minimum period and only when necessary.

67. Furthermore, it is the first Brazilian piece of legislation to discuss the concept of personal data and data processing:

> Article 14. For the purposes of the provisions of this Decree, it is considered:
>
> I — personal data—data related to the identified or identifiable natural person, including identifying numbers, location data or electronic identifiers, when these relate to a person; and
>
> II — personal data processing—any operation performed with personal data, such as those relating to the collection, production, reception, classification, use, access, reproduction, transmission, distribution, processing, archiving, storage, elimination, evaluation or control of the information, modification, communication, transfer, dissemination or extraction.

68. Therefore, this is historically important because it shows the relevancy of data protection.

Chapter 4. Other Relevant National Legal Provisions Regarding the Protection of Privacy

69. The Consumer Defend Code is a relevant legislation when the data subject is a consumer. Another important law is the "great credit score" law.

70. As mentioned in Part 1, the Brazilian Constitution of 1988 has created an action that allows data subjects to have access to their data processed by Public Administration bodies called Habeas Data. To make this operational, a law was enacted to regulate the application of this right. The action, normally, is applied to correct public records. It was the Brazilian beginning of the data subject's right to have correct information about them in databases, a right that now exists in LGPD.

71. Habeas data will be granted:

> I — to ensure knowledge of information relating to the person of the petitioner, contained in the registry or database of government entities or of a public nature;
> II — for the rectification of data, when it is not preferred to do so through confidential, judicial or administrative process;

72. The Consumer Defense Code, as well, is a piece of legislation that has intrinsic relation with data protection since it applies when the data subject is a consumer, as provided for in Article 2 of the Consumer Defense Code:[18]

> Art. 2. A consumer is any physical person or corporate entity who acquires or uses a product or service as a final user.

73. The Consumer Defense Code aims to protect the consumer relationship and, in this regard, imposes on the supplier the need to provide services, as well as to supply products, without flaws or defects, under penalty of civil liability.

74. In this sense, if there are defects related to the provision of service or insufficiency in the information provided to the consumer, the suppliers are legally responsible, according to the discipline set out in Article 14.

75. Article 14. The service supplier will be responsible, regardless of the existence of guilt, for providing the necessary reparations for the damage caused to consumers due to any defects pertaining to service provision, as well as for insufficient or inadequate information about the nature of the service and the risks involved. § 1. The service is deemed defective when it does not provide the safety level expected by the consumer, taking into consideration relevant circumstances such as:

18. Brazil, Consumer's Right Act, Law No. 8.708, Sep. 11, 1990, 1990.

I — the way it was supplied;
II — the results and risks reasonably expected from it;
III — the date when it was provided.

76. From the moment the data controller or data processor handles the personal data of a consumer inappropriately, in any way, onerous or not, there could be a failure in the provision of service. There could be a breach in the consumer's expectation when its data should be safe and used only to carry out what was established in the consumer contract.

77. Although, in order to be eligible for receiving any kind of compensation for the caused damage, it must have been proven that the cause of the damage originated from the company that provides the service. That is to say, it is necessary that clear evidence exists that the damage occurred because of either a failure in the provision of the service by the company, for example, when it suffers a security incident or when it processes the subject's data for illegal or not authorized purposes.

78. Another law that has a great impact on data protection, Federal Law No. 12,414/2011, which deals with the "positive record" and aims to share with institutions interested in carrying out credit analysis to meet consumer demand data that demonstrates "good payer" profile, in other words, its history of payment obligations.

79. It is established the understanding of the legislation in the sense that the registration has an exclusive purpose.

80. Article 5 The registered rights are:

VII — have your personal data used only in accordance with the purpose for which they were collected.

81. Therefore, the purpose of registering consumer data in the "positive bureau" and in the "good payer registration" is solely and exclusively to certify the consumer's reliability in the payment of their debts, and access is given to institutions with the purpose of accessing/consulting the consumer's credit history, to support the decision of granting or not credit/financing, etc.

82. The Brazilian Superior Court of Justice has decided in the same sense:[19]

> SPECIAL APPEAL. CONSUMER. TERMINATION OF DEFENSE. NO OCCURRENCE. CREDIT CARD CONTRACT. ABUSIVE CLAUSES. SHARING PERSONAL DATA. NEED TO OPTION FOR YOUR NEGATIVE. DISREGARD TO THE PRINCIPLES OF TRANSPARENCY AND TRUST. SCOPE OF THE SENTENCE. ATREINTES. REASONABLE. (...)

19. STJ, REsp 1,348,532—SP, Min. Rel. Luís Felipe Salomão, 4th T, DJ: Oct. 10, 2017.

3. It is an abusive and illegal clause provided for in a credit card service agreement, which authorizes the contracting bank to share consumer data with other financial entities, as well as with entities that maintain positive and negative records of consumers, without it being given the option to disagree with that share.
4. The clause included in the credit card service contract that imposes the consent with the sharing of the consumer's personal data is abusive because it fails to meet two important principles of the consumer relationship: transparency and trust.
5. The impossibility of contracting the credit card service, without the option of denying the sharing of consumer data, reveals exposure that makes them indisputably vulnerable, in a way that is impossible to measure and project.
6. In fact, the exposure of your financial data opens up the possibility for various intrusions into the consumer's life. Their habits are known, their way of living and the way they spend expenses are monitored. Therefore, the indispensability of real and spontaneous authorization for the exhibition.
7. The highlighted clause is considered abusive also because the obligation it announces is not necessary for the execution of the contracted service, which is to obtain credit by means of a card.
8. Abusiveness does not extend, of course, to the registration of the name and CPF of any debtors in negative consumer records (SPC, SERASA, among others), due to default, since such measure is supported by law (Law no. 8.078/1990, articles 43 and 44). (...)
11. Special appeal partially provided.

83. Such understanding of the Superior Court of Justice (STJ) gives full effect to Federal Law No. 12.414/2011, considering that the right and, therefore, the consumer's option to register or not always arise from the legal text.

84. On the subject, even the Courts of Justice have judged[20] following the same ratio decidendi originated in STJ:

UNNOMINATED APPEAL. INDEMNITY ACTION FOR PAIN AND MATERIAL DAMAGES. TRANSFER OF PERSONAL INFORMATION AND BANK DATA TO OTHER COMPANIES BY THE TELEPHONE COMPANY. UNDUE CHARGES MADE ON THE CREDIT CARD OF THE COMPLAINT. REFUND OF DEBT, DOUBLE, DUE. ABUSIVE CONDUCT. MORAL DAMAGE. INDEMNITY AMOUNT MAINTAINED. APPEAL KNOWN AND DENIED.

1. In casu, it was shown that after the transfer of personal data and banking information of consumers by the telephone company to the bank, without prior authorization, the claimant was charged on her credit card for unsolicited services.

20. TJPR, 0002916-31.2014.8.16.0184/0, Mag. Report. Renata Ribeiro Bau, 3rd TR, Dj: Oct. 15, 2015.

2. Under these conditions, given the abusive conduct of the defendants, it is due to repeat the undue payment, in double, since bad faith and the intention to obtain undue profit in damages to consumers, as well as compensation for pain and suffering, in the insofar as the situation went beyond the mere collection of debt

85. Moreover, with regard to data protection, Brazil also has the Public Information Access Bill (Law No. 12,527/2011), which regulates the procedures to be observed by the Federal Union, States, Federal District and Municipalities, to guarantee access to information that are in their power. It follows a global initiative to provide more transparency to Public Administration acts. It is an important piece of legislation regarding data protection since it empowers data subjects in contrast to Public Administration.

86. First, it must be considered that The Public Information Access Bill establishes that personal information is one related to an identified or identifiable natural person, the same concept as in Directive 95/46/CE in the GDPR and in LGPD.

87. Additionally, there is a main rule with reference to data protection, which is Article 31:

> Art. 31. The treatment of personal information must be done in a transparent manner and with respect for intimacy, private life, honor and people's image, as well as individual freedoms and guarantees.

88. It is natural that access to information confronts data protection. That is why this rule is so important in terms of data privacy. The law does not only empower data subjects vis-à-vis Public Administration but also puts limits on third parties trying to access information. It creates a balance between access and data protection. These limits are created through a close list of hypotheses in which third parties without data subject consent may have access to the information.

89. § 3 The consent referred to in item II of § 1 will not be required when the information is required:

> I — prevention and medical diagnosis, when the person is physically or legally incapable, and for use solely and exclusively for medical treatment;
> II — carrying out statistics and scientific research of evident public or general interest, provided for by law, the identification of the person to which the information refers being prohibited;
> III — compliance with a court order;
> IV — the defense of human rights; or
> V — preponderant public and general interest protection of the.

90. Furthermore, because it allows access to other people's data, it is different from Habeas Data Law.

91. There are also some pieces of legislation in specific areas, for example, criminal and banking.

92. In criminal area, there is law 12, 737/2012 called "Lei Carolina Dieckman," which establishes some new conducts that constitute crimes like invading an electronic device, altering/destroying data without subject consent or installing vulnerabilities in electronic devices.

93. Article 154-A. Invading someone else's computer device, connected or not to the computer network, by improperly violating a security mechanism and in order to obtain, tamper with or destroy data or information without the express or tacit authorization of the device holder or install vulnerabilities to obtain an illicit advantage.

94. It is called "Carolina Dieckman" because this famous actress had her email hacked. The hacker had access to personal photos and asked for BRL 10,000 not to publish them. The actress refused to pay, and the photos were published on the Internet.

95. Until then, the crimes that occurred in the digital sphere were not considered a crime if they did not resemble crimes from the physical world.

96. In the Brazilian legal system, the bank secrecy law can be found, which guarantees secrecy in banking operations, Supplementary Law 105/2001. The law establishes the hypothesis in which it is not necessary to have subject consent to access it to evade fraud, for example. Consequently, it is an important balance between data protection and access to information. This law also talks about the data subject expressing consent in order for other people to access his/her personal finance data.

97. § 3 It does not constitute a breach of the duty of secrecy:

> V — the disclosure of confidential information with the express consent of the interested parties

98. There is also an important resolution from the National Monetary Council, which encompasses data protection norms, which is Resolution No. 4893. The resolution establishes that financial institutions must have a cybersecurity policy assuring data integrity, disposability, and confidentiality. It must be constituted a plan for data breaches. Finally, it establishes requirements to contract cloud computing, especially outside the Brazilian territory.

99. Article 2. The institutions referred to in Article 1 must implement and maintain a cybersecurity policy based on principles and guidelines that seek to ensure the confidentiality, integrity and availability of the data and information systems used.

100. Article 6. The institutions referred to in Article 1 shall establish an incident action and response plan aimed at implementing the cyber security policy.

101. Article 11. The institutions referred to in Article 1 shall ensure that their policies, strategies and structures for risk management provided for in the regulations in force, specifically with regard to the decision criteria regarding the outsourcing of services, contemplate the contracting of relevant data processing and storage and cloud computing services, in the country or abroad.

102. Article 16. The contracting of relevant processing, data storage and cloud computing services provided abroad must comply with the following requirements:

> I — the existence of an agreement for the exchange of information between the Central Bank of Brazil and the supervisory authorities of the countries where the services may be provided;
> II — the contracting institution must ensure that the provision of the services referred to in the caput does not cause damage to its regular functioning or hinder the performance of the Central Bank of Brazil;
> III — the contracting institution must define, prior to contracting, the countries and regions in each country where the services can be provided and the data can be stored, processed and managed; and
> IV — the contracting institution must provide alternatives for the continuity of the business, in case of impossibility of maintenance or termination of the service provision contract.

103. Recently, another piece of finance legislation related to data protection was enacted. It is the resolution between the Brazilian Central Bank and the National Monetary Council, which refers to the regulation of Open Banking in Brazil. It has some relevant norms related to data protection; for example, it establishes three requirements for data sharing.

104. Article 8. The request to share registration data and transactions and services referred to in Article 5, items I, items "c" and "d," and item II, item "a," comprises the steps of consent, authentication, and confirmation:

- Consent: it cannot be obtained in subscription contracts.
- Authentication: it must have controls to authenticate the data-sharing operation.
- Confirmation: data subject must confirm one's intention to share.

105. Finally, LGPD (Brazilian Data Protection Law) establishes that it is necessary to take security measures to protect personal data. In this perspective, there is the Brazilian Cyber Security Strategy (Decree 10.222/2020—E-cyber); it establishes that Brazil should enhance its mechanisms for managing risks through national cyber governance to reduce vulnerabilities. E-Cyber guides Brazilian society on the main actions of the federal government, in national and international terms, in cybersecurity area in the 2020-2023 quadrennium.

106. All these directives, however, already originated in the Political Charter of 1988, the Major Law of the Republic, and are arranged in a hierarchically binding manner.

Part II. National Data Protection Law

Chapter 1. Background: General of the Brazilian Data Protection Law and Other Similar Relevant National Legislation

107. Construction of the Brazilian Data Protection Law. Citizen Constitution and Consumer Code. Habeas Data. Dividing the law into two.

108. Talking about the construction of Law No. 13.709/18 (Brazilian Data Protection Law) is like talking about a book with many chapters since it has been one of the laws that dwelled for a long period to its total enforcement. It is not simple to talk about the historical trends that might have happened because it is still something new in contrast to other cultures around the world, especially compared to American and European regulations. However, when it comes to legislation trends, it all began with the Brazilian Constitution of 1988, known as the "Citizen Constitution," because it reflects, after a long period of dictatorship, values that were lost and directly associated with a democracy. Not only that but also other regulations that followed with the constitution, such as the Consumer Code, the Habeas Data instrument that came with the Constitution, later regulated by Law No. 9.507/97, those instruments expressed the exercising of data protection rights before the data protection law came upon, not as profound but it could be considered the very first manifestations of data protection rights in Brazil's legal system.

109. The Brazilian Constitution of 1988, regarding ideas relevant to data protection, brought the freedom of speech and the right to be informed, along with the principle of privacy, as, for example, violation of intimacy.[21] Although these principles might bring a notion that would suffice the right to data protection, they are not; since the constant disruption of technologies,[22] only one precise right would be possible to follow the modern setup of informational flows.[23] Analyzing that, the proposal (Constitutional Amendment Proposal—PEC) No. 17/2019, approved

21. Danilo Doneda, *Da Privacidade à Proteção de Dados Pessoais* 260 (Thomson Reuters Brasil 2d ed. 2020).
22. Klaus Schwab, *The Fourth Industrial Revolution* 7 (World Economic Forum 2016–).
23. Danilo Doneda, *Da Privacidade à Proteção de Dados Pessoais* 263 (Thomson Reuters Brasil 2d ed. 2020).

recently,[24] made the right to data protection a fundamental one, being inserted in the list of fundamental rights in Article 5 of the Constitution and Article 22.[25]

110. Law No. 8.078/1990, known as the Consumer Code, has brought new advances in the Brazilian legal order by acknowledging modern rights, especially establishing a balance between the consumer and the provider of the product or service. The Brazilian Consumer Code brought up knowledge towards limiting the usage of the consumer's information, as in the case of maintaining the registration of bad credit score for not longer than a period of five years, besides other rights, as to access their information, correct it and justified cancelation;[26] or as in the definition of database and consumer registration in its Article 43,[27] by defining it as any dataset that might interfere in the free will of the consumer's personality.[28] Although this regulation brought up much innovation, it was not enough to embrace all data protection rights and principles; one example would be as automatized decision-making, which is not something covered by this regulation.

111. As mentioned, the Habeas Data institution is a data protection right predecessor way to exercise it. Being regulated by Law No. 9.507/97, it gives some concepts and procedures to be followed that are somehow similar to the Brazilian Data Protection Law. Nevertheless, this instrument was not enough to cater to every need that has emerged with the advance of the usage of databases of data subjects; for instance, this mechanism could only be used in cases of databases that were from governmental entities or that were mainly public.[29]

112. The need for a specific data protection law was clear, but it was not easy to have it in the Brazilian legal scope. The last chapters for the implementation of this data protection legislation lasted longer than imagined. Created in 2018, the law was supposed to be in full enforcement in 2019. Many propositions have come to delay it. One of them worked, especially because of the COVID-19 Pandemic. The Project of Law No. 1179/2020, which was converted into Law No. 14.010/2020,[30] said that its enforcement was postponed to August 1, 2020, but with an aspect that is unusual when it comes to laws and their pathway to enforcement: while the rights to data protection were immediately inferred on the citizens, and businesses or people that

---

24. Available at https://www.gov.br/anpd/pt-br/assuntos/noticias/senado-federal-aprova-proposta-de-emenda-a-constituicao-17-pec-17-2019-que-inclui-a-protecao-de-dados-pessoais-no-rol-de-direitos-e-garantias-fundamentais#:~:text=O%20Senado%20aprovou%20na%20quarta,de%20legislar%20sobre%20o%20tema (accessed Nov. 7, 2021).
25. Available at https://www25.senado.leg.br/web/atividade/materias/-/materia/135594 (accessed Nov. 7, 2021).
26. Danilo Doneda, *Da Privacidade à Proteção de Dados Pessoais* 264 (Thomson Reuters Brasil 2d ed. 2020–).
27. Brazil, Consumer's Right Act, Law No. 8.708, Sep. 11, 1990, 1990.
28. Bruno R. Bioni, *Proteção de dados pessoais: a função e os limites do consentimento* 12 (Forense 2d ed. 2020).
29. Danilo Doneda, *Da Privacidade à Proteção de Dados Pessoais* 268 (Thomson Reuters Brasil 2d ed. 2020).
30. Available at http://www.planalto.gov.br/ccivil_03/_ato2019-2022/2020/lei/L14010.htm. (Accessed December 10, 2021).

process data for profit were expected to comply with is as well, the administrative sanctions and fines would only be applicable after another year, effectively meaning that two separate deadlines for application applied: one for rights and one for sanctions. There were other attempts of trying to postpone it, but finally, the LGPD (Lei Geral de Proteção de Dados—Brazilian General Data Protection Law) is in full enforcement.[31]

113. Using personal data for different purposes is an undeniable trend, but this material refers to something intrinsic to people and could not be used for purposes without clarification and transparency. That is why the Brazilian Data Protection Law has as its goal to bring protection to personal data and reinforce the informational autonomy and dignity of the data subjects; with that, democracy can be solidified.[32] With a new law like this, a new complex and wide diversity of concepts were brought to the Brazilian legal system, besides its wide applicability, which is going to be presented next.

31. For more information about the law's timeline: https://www.serpro.gov.br/lgpd/menu/arquivos/linha-do-tempo-1/view. Access on Nov. 25, 2021.
32. Ana Frazão, *Lei Geral de Proteção de Dados e suas Repercussões no Direito Brasileiro* 13 (Thomson Reuters Brasil 1st ed. 2019–).

Chapter 2. Material, Personal and Territorial Scope of the Brazilian Data Protection Law

114. It is in the very beginning of the text of the law that it might be found the first manifestation of the scope of the Brazilian Data Protection Law, which says:

> Article 1. This Law provides for the processing of personal data, including in digital media, by a natural person or by a legal entity governed by public or private law, in order to protect the fundamental rights of freedom and privacy and the free development of the natural person's personality.[33]

115. First, as the article above demonstrates, it is necessary to acknowledge that the Brazilian Data Protection Law is applicable for only data that is considered personal, which means that, connecting with the concept of personal data given by the regulation, that is identified information or information that might identify a data subject,[34] other kinds of data that do not reflect information from a person, cannot be considered personal data and be part of the Brazilian data protection law scope.

116. As it follows, in the second part of the article, the law mirrors the intelligence that levels of security for physical documents should have been implemented before. It is possible to infer that when analyzing "including digital media." The reason for this idea is that this law is not just applicable to digital media but also applicable to the ones that are considered physical, such as in printed material and also physical media that might not be understood as well, e.g., pen drivers.

117. The next part, the third one, presents the article as to whom the law may be applied, which are natural people or legal entities, and the last one is associated with public institutions. It is important to mention that this part of the first article connects with other ones from the law.

118. Initially, when it comes to the enforcement of the law, conditions are considered for its applicability, which are identified in Article 3 as follows:

> Article 3 (…)
>
> I — the treatment operation is carried out in the national territory
> II — the processing activity has as its objective the offer or supply of goods or services or the processing of data of individuals located in the national territory; or
> III — the personal data object of the processing has been collected in the national territory.

33. Brazil, Brazilian Data Protection Law (LGPD). Law No. 18.709, Aug. 14, 2018, 2018. Art. 1.
34. *Ibid.*, Art. 5, item II.

119. This means that the law is not bound to the citizenship or nationality of the personal data or its owner,[35] or even who is taking care of the processing, though it is worried about the processing activity and its goal and if it has been collected in the national territory.[36]

120. Although it is necessary to understand that this law adopted the idea of extraterritoriality,[37] which would consider no boundaries to the processing of data that has been collected in national territory, by service or product sale; this means that if the information of the data subject has been collected in Brazilian territory, and the provider of the product is located in a foreign country, then the Brazilian Data Protection Law will be applicable.

121. By the end of the first article, the law ensures its compromise with the fundamental rights of freedom, privacy and free development of the natural person that shows the alignment of the law itself to its principles presented in the following articles.

122. It is also important to bring the non-scope of application of the law, which must not be applicable when the process is done by a natural person without profitable goals; also for academic purposes, if observed the legal purposes for it mentioned in the Articles 7 and 11; exclusively for journalistic and artistic purposes, besides when the personal data is processed for public security and national defense purposes, pursuant to Article 4, I, II, III and IV.[38]

---

35. Patricia Peck Pinheiro, *Personal Data Protection: Comments on Law n. 13.709/2018* 22 (Editora SaraivaJur 3d ed. 2021).
36. According to the first paragraph of the Art. 3, it will be considered personal data those collected in national territory where the data subject might be found in the moment of the collection.
37. Patricia Peck Pinheiro, *Personal Data Protection: Comments on Law n. 13.709/2018* 22 (Editora SaraivaJur 3d ed. 2021).
38. *Ibid.*

Chapter 3. Concepts and Definitions of the Brazilian Data Protection Law

123. For a better understanding of the Brazilian Data Protection Law, it is undeniable that understanding the main terms mentioned in the whole body of law is necessary. Foreseeing this necessity, the legislator brought Article 5, which fulfills many of the new terms that emerged with this law and is spread in its structure. The article was divided into nineteen items to explain the most important terms. To make it simple in this monograph, only for academic purposes, it was decided to divide them into four categories: primary fundamental concepts, secondary fundamental concepts, action-related fundamental concepts, and entities fundamental concepts.

§1. Primary Fundamental Concepts

124. In this section, the concepts of personal data, personal sensitive data, anonymized data and databases are presented.

125. To understand personal data, it would be interesting to first go back a few steps and consider its definition according to Information Security intelligence; in its case, data is a simple unity of content that is associated with a context, becomes information and might acquire value.[39]

126. Therefore, for data to be in the scope of the Brazilian data protection law, it needs to refer to a person.

127. Therefore, personal data for the Brazilian Data Protection Law would be considered any information about a data subject or information that might identify it. At first, some information, such as the color of a t-shirt and the usage of a particular clothing style, might not be considered personal data. However, if this information is inserted in a specific context (e.g., referring to someone's clothing style, as mentioned in a meeting), it could be considered personal data because it will be possible to identify that person (data subject). That is why the concept of personal data, according to the law, is quite vast.

128. On the contrary, the concept of personal sensitive data is completely restricted to what is present in item II, which are: personal data on racial or ethnic origin, religious conviction, political opinion, affiliation to a union or organization of a religious, philosophical or political nature, data referring to health or sexual life, genetic or biometric data, when linked to a natural person.[40]

39. Jule Hintzbergen et al., *Fundamentos Segurança da Informação* 55 (Brasport 3d ed. 2018).
40. Brazil, Brazilian Data Protection Law (LGPD). Law No. 18.709, Aug. 14, 2018, 2018. Art. 5, item II.

129. Differing these two concepts in sensitive or not is a reflection of the different treatment the law gives to each one, as is the case in the hypothesis (legal basis) of processing these data, in which it won't be possible to use consent for the processing of personal sensitive data.

130. Besides these two first fundamental definitions, there is the definition of anonymized data and database.

131. Personal data that has gone through an effective process of anonymization would be considered anonymized data. The law also defines what is considered anonymization, which will be presented in the following part of this chapter, but it simply could be considered as applying the action that removes any binding there might be between the data subject and the personal data using reasonable and available technical means, meaning that the context of being "personal" would not exist anymore; consequently, there would be no more personal data and hence no enforcement of the law for this anonymized data.

132. Ending the primary fundamental concepts, database is any structured set of personal data established in one or several places, in electronic or physical support.[41] It is worthy to mention one specification brought by the law that refers to a "structured database" and the diversity of places mentioned.

133. A structured database might be one that has a previous context that determines its structure, as in the case of a table that requests specific contexts to be filled in by someone or something (e.g., A table in Excel), while a nonstructured database would be the ones without this previous context, not following a rule or any kind of organization (e.g., Images, voice records, etc.). Understanding this part is important to what comes when law refers to its concept related to its safety, as the law requires in Article 49.

134. With the advance of cloud services, it is quite common that the location of the data centers is not on national ground. Nevertheless, if these databases are in other places, but the prerequisites already mentioned (territory, material and personal scope) are fulfilled, they are going to have the enforcement of the Brazilian Data Protection Law. Overall, it also should be reminded that data which is physical means (e.g., printed material), is included in this matter.

§2. Secondary Fundamental Concepts

135. In this part, the definitions of data subject, agents of processing, controller, processor and data manager are explained.

41. *Ibid.*, Art. 5, item IV.

136. The Brazilian Data Protection Law clearly defines who would be considered a data subject, the natural person to whom the processed data relate. Still, it is important to mention who would be considered a natural person in the Brazilian legal order.[42]

137. The Brazilian Civil Rights Code defines a natural person as a subject of rights and obligations who was born alive and has the capacity to exert the act of civil life.[43] It is not intended to go further in the construction of this concept since it is a specific construction of Civil Rights, and it is not the main purpose to discuss it here. It is important to mention here that the rights given by the Brazilian Data Protection Law are not applicable to people who have already passed away.

138. The agents of processing in the national data protection law are defined as two: Controller and Processor.

139. The Controller, as it said in item VI of Article 5, must be considered any natural person or legal one, from private or public law, from which competes the decisions taken with personal data.[44] The main essence of defining the Controller position is to understand that this agent of processing has the power to decide what to do with the personal data, including sharing it with another agent to process it in the Controller's name, which will be the Processor.

140. It is important to mention that natural people can be considered Controllers; it might sound unusual at first, but if a natural person has in the processing activity of personal data the main goal to profit, and in its realm, it is responsible for the decision-making, this natural person must be considered as a Controller.

141. The Processor, defined by the law, has the same structure (natural and legal person; private or public law), but the main difference resides in the fact that the processor has no decision-making power, which will be restricted to what it has agreed to be done with the Controller.

142. It is quite common to see in the processing activating the figure of a Processor treating data taking its own decision-making with personal data. That's why other figures can emerge from these different ways of processing data. Seeing that, the Brazilian Data Protection National Authority decided to launch a manual to indicate other agents beyond the ones the law acknowledges.

---

42. *Ibid.*, Art. 5, item V.
43. Brazil, Brazilian Civil Code. Law No. 10.406, Jan. 10, 2002, 2002. Arts. 1–3.
44. Brazil, Brazilian Data Protection Law (LGPD). Law No. 18.709, Aug. 14, 2018, 2018. Art. 5°, item VI.

143. With this publication, the division branches from both Controller and Processor were accredited as Joint Controllers (including independent one) and Subprocessor.[45]

144. It should be taken into consideration that it was decided to call "Data Manager" instead of "DPO" to bring into knowledge that the Brazilian Data Protection Law decided to bring another term, and as a literal translation from Portuguese to English, it would be "Data Manager," although the term "DPO" has really become usual in the common dialogues about that protection in Brazil, especially because that the Brazilian figure resembles the one from the GDPR.

145. Then, the Brazilian Data Manager, as defined by item VIII from Article 5, should be a person that can be indicated by either the Controller or the Processor to act as a point of contact between the Controller, data subjects, and the Brazilian National Authority.[46]

146. Other attributions mentioned to the position of the Brazilian Data Manager would as to accept the complaints and communication of the data subjects by clearing any doubts and take steps if required; guide employees and hired ones from the organization about the measures to be taken in relation to the personal data; execute other designations determined by the Controller or established in complementary norms.

147. It should be remembered that the Brazilian Data Protection Law does not many make any references to the Data Manager's education, but they will be working with a complex law, technology, management and communication, besides finding a person with all these knowledge and skills can be a daunting task;[47] then there would be a possibility of having the kind of service demanded to a Data Manager by an organization attended by another organization—DPO as a Service.

§3. ACTION-RELATED FUNDAMENTAL CONCEPTS

148. In this part, it was decided to call it "action related" because most of the concepts in this part are related to something considered an "action of something which is done or performed," as in the case of the definition of "data processing." The other ones that are going to be presented as well are: anonymization, consent, blocking, elimination, international transfer, shared usage and DPIA.

45. For more, consult: https://www.gov.br/anpd/pt-br/assuntos/noticias/anpd-publica-guia-de-seguranca-para-agentes-de-tratamento-de-pequeno-porte. Access on Nov. 5, 2021.
46. Brazil, Brazilian Data Protection Law (LGPD). Law No. 18.709, Aug. 14, 2018, 2018. Art. 5º, item VIII.
47. L.R. Garcia, *Lei Geral de Proteção de Dados (LGPD): Guia de implantação* 19 (Editora Blucher 2020).

149. Everything that might be done with personal data would be considered data processing, especially because the law brought up twenty verbs to exemplify what would be considered data processing (e.g., collection, production, reception, etc.), so this concept is extensive.[48]

150. As mentioned before, anonymization would be the action of removing the binding between the data subject and its personal data, using reasonable and available technical means. And if the anonymization method was effective, there would not be personal data anymore. There are many methods of anonymization, such as generalization and randomization, but talking about them is not the main goal of this article.

151. It is important to mention that the text of the law brought up the idea of reasonable meaning to reduce the extension of the concept of personal data and avoid crossing the border between personal data and anonymized data.[49]

152. The Brazilian Data Protection Law, when it comes to the concept of consent, has brought up great points to its definition as being a free manifestation, informed and unmistakable for one determined goal. For a better understanding of consent in the Brazilian Data Protection Law, some parts of its concept are divided.

153. First, a free manifestation would be one in which the data subject is able to analyze the options given to themselves, being able to freely choose either having or not having their personal data processed for that specific processing activity; consequently, we might find a granularity of this consent. It is important to check the asymmetry of power, as Bioni says:

> The central issue is always to check the existence of some type of subordination—power asymmetry—that can undermine the voluntariness of consent, and there should be a case-by-case analysis to conclude whether consent can be classified as free or not. (Bioni, 2021, p. 189).

154. Second, which already connects with a previous part mentioned, the data subject needs to be informed and not only deliver the message but make it clear and accessible to the data subjects' expertise. The data flow needs to be transparent to the data subject, as said by Bioni:

> It is worth repeating, the provision of information is only reasonable if it causes transparency in the flow of personal data. This is the optimal expected result arising from the satisfactory fulfillment of the duty to inform and, ultimately, of what is expected when adjectivizing consent as informed. (Bioni, 2021, p. 188).

48. Brazil, Brazilian Data Protection Law (LGPD). Law No. 18.709, Aug. 14, 2018, 2018. Art. 5°, item X.
49. Bruno Ricardo Bioni, *Proteção de Dados Pessoais: A Função e os Limites do Consentimento* 66 (Grupo GEN 3d ed. 2021–).

155. Third, consent needs to be unmistakable, which tells that the action of the data subject will be shown directly and in an explicit form; the silence of the data subject cannot be considered a demonstration of agreement. This point of consent is tightly connected with the goal/end of data processing because the Brazilian Data Protection Law defines the principle of purpose, which defines that the processing of data needs to have clear goals, specific, explicit and informed to the data subject, without the possibility of processing in an incompatible for after the end of the processing goal:

> Any declaration must have a direction, as it is not allowed in a vacuum and in a generic way. It would be the equivalent of issuing a kind of "blank check" that would empty any sphere of citizen's control over their data. In practical terms, the famous "for the purpose of improving your experience," contained in numerous privacy policies, should be abandoned. (Bioni, 2020, p. 190)

156. After this study of consent, the discussion about it is wide, and at this moment is not the scope of this chapter.

157. As it follows the category defined here of action-related fundamental concepts, there is the concept of blocking, which is defined as the temporary suspension of any data processing by guarding the personal data or the database.[50] Its concept is simple to be understood, although it is necessary that this fact might happen for a manifestation of the data subject by exerting its right, or it can happen if a violation happens, and the ANPD decides so according to the law.

158. The other concept this category has is the act of elimination, which is considered the deletion of personal data or a group of it stored in a database, besides not mattering the procedure applied.[51] It is important to mention that this is an irreversible act because after the deletion of the data. It is also important to understand that this concept is different from the right of being forgotten, which has not been adopted by the Brazilian legal system, considering it incompatible with the Constitution.[52]

159. International transfer is considered the act of transferring to a foreign country or international body in which the country is a member.[53] The concept is quite clear to determine what this action would is considered, but the Brazilian Data Protection Law has brought up a full chapter with many conditions for international transfer.[54]

---

50. Brazil, Brazilian Data Protection Law (LGPD). Law No. 18.709, Aug. 14, 2018, 2018. Art. 5, item XIII.
51. *Ibid*, Art. 5, item XIV.
52. Portal STF. Brazil. STF conclui que direito ao esquecimento é incompatível com a Constituição Federal. Available at https://portal.stf.jus.br/noticias/verNoticiaDetalhe.asp?idConteudo=460414&ori=1. Access on December 6, 2021.
53. Brazil, Brazilian Data Protection Law (LGPD). Law No. 18.709, august 14th, 2018. 2018. Article 5, XV.
54. *Id.*, Ch. V. of International Transfer of Data.

160. As it follows, the concept of shared usage of data is quite simple, which is considered to be the communication, diffusion, international transfer, and interconnection of personal data or shared processing by organs or public entities in the accomplishment of the legal competences between public entities and private ones, with reciprocity, with specific authorization, for one or more processing allowed by public entities, or private ones.[55] A great example to understand clearer this example would be the usage of shared data in diplomatic relations.

161. To end this category, the definition of DPIA follows as a document from the controller which contains the description of the data processing that might generate risks to civil liberties and fundamental rights, as well as measures to safeguard mechanisms of risk mitigation.[56] This document can either be requested by the Brazilian National Authority of Data Protection when the processing of personal data is based on the legitimate interest of the Controller[57] or whenever it understands its necessity.

162. There is still much to be defined by the Brazilian National Authority of Data Protection when it comes to the Brazilian "DPIA," although it tends to follow the structure of the one from the GDPR although:

> Despite, therefore, a system of co-regulation, through the principle of accountability, is a trend that brings the Brazilian model closer to the European one; the difference surrounding not only the normative framework in question, but also mainly the socioeconomic context in which they will be applied, must be kept in mind. Thus, any equivalence between the Brazilian and European regulatory framework tends to be calibrated by the actions of the future Brazilian Personal Data Protection Authority, as subsequent regulations will signal more precisely what space will be occupied by such co-regulation tools and, ultimately, analysis, how the principle of accountability will come to life. (Bioni & Schertel, 2019, p. 19)[58]

§4. Entities Fundamental Concepts

163. In this part, the concept of researching bodies and the Brazilian ANPD will be defined.

164. As defined in item IX from Article 5, researching bodies are bodies or entities from public administration, direct or indirect, or legal persons of private law

55. *Id.*, Art. 5, XVI.
56. *Id.*, Art. 5, VII.
57. *Id.*, Art. 10, para. 3.
58. Bruno R. Bioni & Laura M. Schertel, *Regulamento Europeu de Proteção de Dados Pessoais e a Lei Geral brasileira de Proteção de Dados: mapeando convergências na direção de um nível de equivalência* (Publisher Revista dos Tribunais 2020). Revista dos Tribunais.

without any profit goals that have been legally built under Brazilian law, with headquarters and forum in the country, and its mission must be institutional, or its objective should be social or statutory to basic research applied with historical, scientific, technological or statistical character. It is important to mention that, as a good practice, while processing data, especially sensitive data, these bodies should do them by anonymizing them; this is mentioned in one of the legal bases of data processing, in Article 7, item IV and Article 11, item II, letter "c"; which indicate that as much as possible, the anonymization of personal data when processed by research bodies.[59]

165. The Brazilian ANPD is the body of the public administration responsible for taking care, implementing and policing the fulfillment of the Data Protection Law in the whole national territory.[60] The creation of the Brazilian ANPD comes to two conditions:

> It is possible to say then that the defense of the creation of a National Data Protection Authority replicated, on the one hand, lessons learned from a model of wide international success and, on the other hand, given the Brazilian diagnosis, it attacked problems that were specifically inherent to it. In order to guarantee independence and technique, it aimed to bring together in a single entity a very wide range of functions. On a long, but not exhaustive, list, it saw itself in the potential Authority responsible for standardizing, implementing, formulating, promoting, sanctioning, educating and listening to society. The specific activities that the debate suggested to it ranged from a broad normative-regulatory capacity to auditing and international data transfer management skills.[61] (De Paula & Vasconcelos, 2019, p. 40)

166. The Brazilian National Data Protection law has shown its importance since its very beginning and now is worried about internalizing this new culture to companies and people through the publishing of manuals and recommendations, even with a short body of members.

59. Brazil, Brazilian Data Protection Law (LGPD) Law No. 18.709, Aug. 14, 2018, 2018. Art. 7, item IV.
60. *Ibid.*, Art. 5, item XIX.
61. Beto Vasconcelos & Felipe De Paula, *Lei Geral de Proteção de Dados e suas Repercussões no Direito Brasileiro* 712 (Thomson Reuters Brasil 1st ed. 2019).

Part III. General Principles

167. The General LGPD aims to protect the fundamental rights of freedom and privacy and the free development of the personality of the natural person. It is important to note that this law applies only to data of individuals. With that in mind, LGPD does not have an impact on the data of companies or public and private institutions but rather on data that these legal entities have of individuals. Within these individuals protected by the LGPD, they are employees, partners, customers, and third parties, among others. After this brief summary, this chapter will bring all the principles that guide the LGPD and that are the complement of the legal regulation.

Chapter 1. General Principles of LGPD

168. First, it is important to highlight that, as a concept of natural person, we have the Brazilian Civil Code itself, as mentioned before, having, in its Article 6, that: "The existence of the natural person ends with death; this is presumed, as for the absent, in cases where the law authorizes the opening of definitive succession." Therefore, the LGPD aims to protect personal data of living persons.

169. As it follows, the LGPD itself brings its concept, being given (Article 5, item I) all personal information related to the identified or identifiable natural person, but the law has not been clear as to the meaning of "identifiable," however, based on the GDPR (European data protection regulation), it is possible to define identifiable for this scenario as a natural person that can be identified, directly or indirectly, through some information that may be a name, identification number, location data, electronic identifiers, or other specific elements related to that natural person.

170. This concept is wide so that it can encompass both information that directly identifies a natural person as their full name, Cadastro de Pessoa Física (CPF) number by means of individual registration or individual taxpayer registry in Brazil, and related information of various types.

171. It is also important to bring back the term "Data processing." As presented before, it could be any processing that would basically be the same as the action employed in each personal data, that is, actions involving its collection, production, reception, classification, use, access, reproduction, transmission, distribution, processing, archiving, storage, elimination, evaluation or control of information, modification, communication, transfer, dissemination or extraction (Article 5, item X).

172. In an introductory nature, it is important to point out that any processing should happen in good faith, which means following the related legal principles presented in the scope of the law.

173. Such points are extremely important because, on many occasions, it is necessary that law enforcement uses as a basis the legal principles to assist in connection with the other principles of the entire legal order in cases where there are doubts or conflicts between natural, legal, or, among others, that may occur, situations involving the processing of personal data.

174. When it comes to Legal principles, they represent an expressional category constructed by man according to the values considered important and relevant in society about certain subjects, objects, and the relationships they establish among themselves, thus recognized by the legal order, which bring together, in their surroundings, the statements and legal norms aimed at prescribing conduct and disciplining intersubjective relations.

175. Therefore, knowing principles is equivalent to knowing the essence of the matter under attention, facilitating the dissection of the object under study. Not knowing the principles, on the contrary, would undermine the possibility of investigating and thoroughly knowing the object.

176. Well, from such introductory considerations, to try to facilitate the recognition of good conduct and also of practices that are inadequate in the day-to-day business, the ten guiding principles of the LGPD will be presented, located in its Article 6, which demand those who process data to be compliant with them.

§1. Principle of Purpose (Article 6, Item I)

177. The first principle chosen to be presented, which is one of the tenth presented in the Brazilian Data Protection Law, is the one called "principle of purpose."

178. This principle defines that data should be processed with legitimate, specific, explicit, and informed purposes to the holder. It is important to know that there is no possibility of further treatment that is incompatible with these purposes. Which means if the purpose of that processing is over, the data should not be in the agent of processing's systems or databases anymore.

179. When we talk about legitimate purposes, the law refers to a purpose driven by common sense, reason, legality, good customs and good faith, departing completely from emotional initiative, illicit and bad faith.

180. As for the specific ones, they emphasize that the objective of the treatment is relevant.

181. For explicit purposes, and in other words, it is the objective that needs to be clear and previously outlined, not allowing doubts to arise after the specification of its content.

182. Processing a patient's data for its treatment, exclusively what would be necessary, giving its transparency (which is one principle as well) that is required, could be a good manifestation of compliance to its principle.

183. All these objectives together form the purpose allowed by the LGPD and must be informed to the holder, who is responsible for delimiting the subject matter of the treatment. Any future change in the defined purposes should be made only if the data subject is informed and, depending on its legal basis of processing, it should be informed and have their agreement, i.e., imagine a start-up company that requests the customer's email address for the specific purpose of login on the platform. In this case, you cannot automatically use that same email to send advertising or offers; there is a change in purpose, which would implicate in an infraction not only to the purpose of processing but consequently affect all other requirements.

§2. Adequacy (Article 6, Item II)

184. By this principle, we see that the data processed must be compatible with the needs of the company; that is, its activity should make sense with the data that is collected. For example, if your business is a trade in electronic products, it will hardly be justifiable to request users their health data. Thus, if it is not compatible, the processing, once again, will be acknowledged as inadequate.

185. In other words, the principle of adequacy is explained by the link of conformity established between the treatment and the purpose objectified, as previously informed to the data subject and authorized by them.

§3. Necessity (Article 6, Item III)

186. Data collection, in general, should be performed only in relation to data strictly necessary to achieve its purposes. A balance must be made between what is essential and what is only convenient.

187. Thus, by the principle of necessity, we can understand that there is a limitation of the performance of the processing to the minimum necessary for the accomplishment of its purposes, with the scope of the relevant, proportional, and non-excessive data in relation to the purposes of the data processing.

188. It is worth mentioning that the more data you treat, the greater your responsibility will be, including in cases of data breaches and security incidents.

§4. Free Access (Article 6, Item IV)

189. The principle of free access ensures that the holder of the personal data consults, in a simple and free way, any data that the company holds about them; that is, it is assured to the holders who consult on the form and duration of the processing, and also on the completeness of their personal data.

190. This warranty is valid only if there is express acceptance given by the data subject in the appropriate form and time.

§5. Data Quality (Article 6, Item V)

191. Holders must be assured that the information the company has about them is true and up to date. It is necessary to pay attention to the accuracy, clarity, and relevance of the data according to the need and for the purpose of its treatment.

192. This principle is based on ensuring the accuracy, clarity, relevance and updating of the data subject's data, according to the data processing needs and the achievement of the objectives. Data quality, therefore, is an essential aspect of treatment.

193. In certain cases, when it is brought up to day-to-day processing, a trivial error, e.g., a bank that processed the name of a client while analyzing the person's score to a house mortgage, confuses one part of the name and then gets its request denied, this data processor might be conflicting not only a principle from LGPD but also a social right, the one to housing, presented by the Brazilian Constitution.[62]

194. Accuracy leads us to precision, that is, to the strict link established between data, processing, and purpose. However, clarity is related to the concept that this relationship is based on words and procedures, which undoubtedly clarifies the receipt of messages. Relevance, in turn, indicates that the relevant processing will only be carried out if such procedures allow the purpose of prior objectification and the approval of the data subject has been obtained previously; finally, the update emphasizes what the data requires in a continuous revision.

§6. Transparency (Article 6, Item VI)

195. This principle shows that all the information that a company provides, in all its means of communication, must be clear, true, and accurate.

196. Another important point included in this principle is that for a company to share personal data, it is required to fulfill transparency, which means that the data subject should always be informed about the processing of their data.

197. Transparency deserves to be emphasized since the data subject and his data are the most important elements within a processing procedure.

198. As a concept of transparency in the information, it is important to understand the view that it is to indicate that the use of excessively technical content does not connect with the objective of this principle because what is sought to ensure is that natural people, regardless of the degree of their education, can understand without any difficulties of what the corresponding information is about, especially because, for the whole procedure to occur, it is essential that you are aware of what will happen to your data after you are processed.

---

62. Brazil, Brazil's Federal Constitution, 1988. 1988. Art. 6:

> Art. 6° São direitos sociais a educação, a saúde, a alimentação, o trabalho, a moradia, o transporte, o lazer, a segurança, a previdência social, a proteção à maternidade e à infância, a assistência aos desamparados, na forma desta Constituição.

§7. Security (Article 6, Item VII)

199. Companies, therefore, have the responsibility to seek procedures, technologies, or means that can guarantee the protection of personal data so that third parties do not have access to them improperly.

200. It is important to emphasize that, in addition to this responsibility, it is up to the companies holding personal data to ensure that measures are taken to resolve accidental situations, such as changes, losses and destruction of personal data, that is, when performing the processing of data, and even after that, it is necessary to use technical and administrative measures that are capable of providing protection to the data from any access that is not authorized.

201. Thus, we have that the central point of this principle is the preservation of personal data that is being processed, always in a secure environment.

202. Another relevant point of this principle is that if there is loss, access, or alteration of data resulting from voluntary conduct, or even if it is an accident, it is the protector of this information, mandatorily, the prediction of all hypotheses that may occur, so that they can prevent any type of problem.

§8. Prevention (Article 6, Item VIII)

203. For this principle, it is extremely important that companies take measures to avoid the existence of any damage resulting from the processing of personal data; that is, companies must act in advance to any problem and not after.

204. Despite the concept being inserted in the principle of security, the legislature preferred to impose the prevention expressly, apart, as a reiteration of conduct, that the protection of data during all its processing cycle is a duty imposed on anyone who accesses and disposes of them, being also embraced by the principle of security.

§9. Nondiscrimination (Article 6, Item IX)

205. This principle demands that the personal data processed can never be used as a form of discrimination or abuse of its data subjects.

206. It is true that the LGPD itself has created specific rules for this category of data called sensitive personal data, which include information such as racial, ethnic origin, religion, political opinion, membership of a trade union or religious, philosophical or political organization, data related to health or sexual life, and finally, genetic or biometric data.

207. Then, with ownership, we can say that the LGPD has expressly prohibited the processing of personal data that is, as an end, discriminatory, unlawful, or abusive.

208. It is important to be pointed out that even though a processor might think that discriminatory processing would be just fine if justified by a legal basis of processing. But that would be totally incompatible not only with the Brazilian Data Protection Law but also with all other legal regimes of Brazil, especially the Federal Constitution.

§10. Responsibility and Accountability (Article 6, Item X)

209. Last, but not least, there is the principle of responsibility and accountability, which provides that, in order to demonstrate good faith and diligence, it is necessary to have evidence that all measures have been adopted.

210. As an example of this, we can imagine evidence such as the offer of team training and hiring specialized consultancies; in short, all measures that demonstrate and ensure the security of personal data and also aim at the ease of access of the data subject, whenever necessary.

211. However, as an outcome, it is important to note that, despite the due proof, such measures also need to be effective and in accordance with the data protection standard because, if it's not, even if acted in good faith, it will be the same as the violation of the principle of responsibility and accountability.

212. So, it is concluded, therefore, that the principles brought here are indispensable in the application to concrete cases; of the much contained in the LGPD, their knowledge and mastery are still indispensable for those who wish to act in the world of data protection of natural persons.

Chapter 2. Legal Grounds for Processing Personal Data

213. The legal bases are the hypotheses of the LGPD that authorize the processing of personal data. Each processor, in its activity, must identify the goal of that data processing to link with a legal ground for processing, which means that for each purpose of processing, it must be attached to one of the possibilities indicated by the LGPD.

214. The idea of having legal grounds for processing in the LGPD connects with the principle of lawfulness of processing. Every processing of personal data, where the LGPD is applicable, should be based on a legal justification.

215. As well, it is important to punctuate that there are exemptions for controllers not pointing out one legal basis for processing, which is mentioned in Article 4 of the LGPD. These cases are:

- if carried out by a natural person for exclusively private and noneconomic purposes;
- if carried out for the exclusive purposes:
  (a) journalistic and artistic; or
  (b) academics, applying to this hypothesis Articles 7 and 11 of this Law.
- if carried out for the exclusive purposes of:
  (a) public safety;
  (b) national defense;
  (c) State security; or
  (d) investigation and prosecution of criminal offenses.
- if coming from outside the national territory and which is not the object of communication, shared use of data with Brazilian processing agents or object of international data transfer with another country other than the country of origin, provided that the country of origin provides a degree of protection of personal data appropriate to the provisions of this Law.

216. LGPD has divided the categories of lawful basis for processing, one in Article 7 for personal data and the other in Article 11 for sensitive personal data, which excludes some of the hypotheses presented by Article 7.

217. These legal hypotheses for processing data brought up by the LGPD should be understood as fixed ones, already having those which are much open for interpretation as the Legitimate Interest. As pointed out by Viola and Teffé:

> It is understood that both the role of art. 7 and Art. 11 are exhaustive, being endowed with some more open hypotheses and with a certain degree of subjectivity (such as, for example, legitimate interest). There are, however, authors who defend the existence of another legal basis for the processing of personal data in Art. 23 of the LGPD, for the general exercise of powers or the fulfillment of legal attributions of the Public Administration. (Art. 7, II, and Art. 11,

> II, "a"), since the performance of the Public Administration of a legal commandment, and the treatment and shared use of data can be executed for the execution of public policies (Art. 7, III, and Art. 11, II, "b"). A provision not provided for in art. 23 It would only bring additional and specific requirements for the processing of personal data carried out by the Public Administration, complementing a legal basis selected in art. 7 or 11 of the law. (Viola and Teffé, 2020, p. 132)

218. In the following pages, it will be presented the lawful hypothesis for processing data, that are part of the articles of the LGPD mentioned, Articles 7 and 11.

§1. Data Subject's Consent

219. Consent, as defined by the law itself, and seen before here, is the "free, informed and unequivocal manifestation by which the data subject agrees to the processing of his personal data for a given purpose" (Article 5, inc. XII).

220. The free manifestation, as the nomenclature itself already says, is summarized in the consent must be free; that is, the data subject may not be obliged to consent, and it is not allowed to obtain consent automatically.

221. Interestingly shown by Bioni (2021, p. 188), there is a side of the consent in the Brazilian Data Protection Law that refers to the power of bargain of the data subject, which reflects in the possibility of them understanding the implications of the processing of their data when the consent is applied, and if they are going to accept—since it is consent—or not the processing of their data.

222. The citizen's "bargaining power" must be verified in relation to the treatment of their personal data, which implies considering what the data subject's options are in relation to the type of data collected until its possible uses. In short, the "menu of options" available to citizens will calibrate how free their consent is to the exact extent that this "menu" equalizes such asymmetrical relationship.

223. The data subject should also be anticipated and clearly informed about what he is consenting to at that time and still know the purpose of this collection.

224. It must be clear that the information provided is understandable to all levels of knowledge of society; thus, it would not be acceptable if the processor of the data is from another country, e.g., Greece, while providing services in Brazil, would use a term of consent in Greek instead of Portuguese. As the law itself brought up in Article 9, when it talks about the rights of the data subjects, the processor must provide information in a clear, adequate and wide way about the processing of their information.

225. Article 9. The data subject has the right to facilitated access to information on the processing of his data, which must be made available in a clear, adequate and ostensible way, among other characteristics provided for in regulations, to comply with the principle of free access.

226. Also, as pointed out by Bioni (2021, p. 184):

> "Therefore, information is not just an approximation, but, from such a perspective, it enables the layman to protect themselves. Thus, from a substantial (qualitative) point of view, information must add, must add, must fill the void of informational asymmetry, equalizing it."

227. Finally, there can be no doubt about the veracity of this consent provided by the data subject, and the benefit of the obtainable part is the burden of proof that the respective consent was obtained in accordance with the legal dictates.

228. Thus, consent may be provided in writing or by any other means that demonstrates the will of the data subject if it has a specific purpose and has transparency in its content.

229. Any other misleading, abusive, or uninformed text to the data subject may invalidate the consent obtained. Another point that must be observed is, if the holder wishes to withdraw the consent provided, such an act should be done easily and free of charge.

§2. Compliance with a Legal or Regulatory Obligation by the Controller

230. In this case, there is a law or a normative act that imposes the processing of data, whether for the provision, adequacy, or modification of personal data. That is, there is a legal provision that requires the use of a given action related to that data and is, therefore, not a discretionary choice of companies or agents of treatment.

231. As a current example, imagine a private hospital that collects information from a patient diagnosed with COVID-19 and shares this data with the Ministry of Health. See that, in this example, there is no consent of the patient because the law requires it to be carried out in this way to maintain statistics in favor of public health, according to the text of Ordinance No. 1,792 of the Ministry of Health.

§3. Implementation of Public Policies

232. This item is only applied to Public Administration; that is, it cannot be used as a legal basis for the processing of data from companies that do not belong to state structures. Here, it is necessary to note that Chapter IV of the LGPD regulates the use of personal data by the public authorities in cases of data processing in the execution of public policies.

233. Public policies are understood, programs related to rights guaranteed to citizens, and may be related to the area of education, health, environment, transportation, and housing, among others.

234. Thus, the sharing of data by the public administration, and clear within a context of public policy execution, is another permissive hypothesis, even if there is no specific consent for this purpose.

235. However, there are caveats, and the body that collected the respective data must clearly inform you that it will share this information and with whom it will share such data.

236. On the other hand, the body that will receive the collected data needs to justify this need to receive, based on the execution of a determined public policy, containing the reason for the request for the data and what will be the use of it.

§4. Studies and Research

237. This legal basis applies only to agencies focused on research for the benefit of society.

238. However, whenever possible, it is necessary to ensure the anonymization of personal data through mechanisms that prevent the identification of an individual through one of these collected data, either through encryption or some other anonymizing means.

239. A good example would be a poll to ascertain the voting intentions of an election. Through this, it is possible to verify the proportion of votes for each candidate divided by region, social class, etc. And, even if the final objective of the research is fulfilled, it is impossible to know who were the people who participated in the interview.

§5. Execution of Contracts

240. Another exception that dispenses consent, and one should be very careful about, is when there is a contract signed, it is necessary to use the data of the holder to proceed with the preparation and execution of this contract, and the consent for this occasion is considered tacit, provided that such contract is agreed upon and executed at the request of the holder himself.

241. It can also be an example of this legal basis with the employment contract. As is known, for the conclusion of a work contract, it is necessary to share with the employer the employee's personal data, e.g., full name, CPF, RG, address, CTPS number (work card number), and bank account, among several others.

§6. Exercise of Rights in Judicial, Administrative, or Arbitral Proceedings

242. In the case of judicial, administrative, or arbitral proceedings, the parties have the right to produce evidence against each other, and the protection of personal data does not block this right. Thus, the purpose of this legal basis is to provide an adversarial and broad defense, as well as to ensure due process of law. Therefore, in these situations, the processing of data is authorized in case of court order, legal, contractual, or procedural imposition.

§7. Protection of the Life or Physical Safety of the Holder

243. Here, we have that this legal basis is linked to the state of need of the holder. That is, imagine an individual who suffers an accident, and with it, people who are on site to rescue him will have access to the cell phone or documents of this individual, to assist in communication with the family, call help or even call the health plan.

244. Therefore, in a situation like this, it is possible that the collection and sharing of this personal data for the purposes of protection of the life or physical safety of the holder is carried out within the legal dictates.

§8. Health Protection

245. This legal basis should be allocated in specific situations determined in the Law; that is, it applies to procedures performed by health professionals, health authorities or health services.

246. Imagine a scenario where a person had their health plan adjusted after the operator accessed some health information of the holder. Such a hypothetical situation is an example of what is vetoed by the LGPD, and health plan operators are prohibited from using this data to select customer risks.

247. Because it is exclusive to these hypotheses brought by the LGPD, therefore, the interest of pharmacies, health plan entities and hospitals to violate the protection of data considered sensitive, related to the health of its data subject.

§9. Legitimate Interest of the Controller

248. This legal basis is undoubtedly the one that brings the most controversy in its application, and although unprecedented in Brazilian law, it is constantly used abroad.

249. With this legal basis, the controller is authorized to process personal data for various purposes, even without having the consent of the holder for each of them individually. However, it is worth noting that, to be used, it is necessary to ascertain whether the company's interest in processing the data is proportional to the legitimate expectation of the holder, always aiming to keep intact their fundamental rights and freedoms.

§10. Credit Protection

250. The last legal basis brought by Article 7 can be used by both credit protection agencies and companies to legitimize the processing of personal data of consumers/customers in credit analysis activities and positive registration. Here it seeks to guarantee credit in situations of collection or debts contracted by the holders.

251. Therefore, what is concluded is that none of the legal hypotheses listed preponderates the other ones, so it is necessary to always apply the legal basis that best suits the operation performed by the controller.

252. Thus, it is of paramount importance that companies that use personal data in their *activities* make the adequacy of their compliance policies and internal procedures as soon as possible so that they protect themselves and comply with the Brazilian Data Protection Law, thus ensuring the regularity of their processing operations.

Chapter 3. Special Categories of Personal Data

§1. Special Categories and Differences Between the Processing of Personal Data and Sensitive Personal Data

253. When the law brings up the idea of personal data of children and adolescents, there must be unequivocal consent from the parents or a legal guardian.

254. In addition, the content must be strictly necessary for economic or governmental activity and sharing with third parties is prohibited. If the treatment agent does not have consent for this collection, it may only be allowed for emergency cases, such as contact with parents or guardians for the protection of these minors.

255. However, when we talk about sensitive personal data, it should be emphasized that the law did not bring a prohibition on the processing, but rather greater protection to them to avoid discriminatory acts.

256. According to the law, sensitive data is one that involves:

(a) racial or ethnic origin;
(b) religious conviction;
(c) political opinion;
(d) membership of a trade union or religious organization;
(e) philosophical or political;
(f) data regarding health or sexual life;
(g) genetic or biometric data when linked to a natural person.

257. It is noteworthy that, as the LGPD has, the processing of sensitive data can only be carried out by explicit consent of that subject in the manner provided for Article 5, item XII, which says:

> Art. 5º For the purposes of this Law, it is considered:
>
> > XII — consent: free, informed and unambiguous manifestation by which the holder agrees to the processing of his personal data for a specific purpose;

258. That means whenever sensitive personal data is processed, it is necessary that there is the consent of the holder and a defined purpose. And, in the absence of this authorization, the processing will only be allowed in situations related to legal quarrels; public policies; research studies; a right, in contract or process; the preservation of a person's life and physical integrity; the protection of procedures performed by health or health professionals; prevention of fraud against the holder.

259. With these two concepts in mind, it is extremely valuable that the processing of sensitive personal data should be carried out with utmost caution because if there is any security incident with this data category, it can seriously affect the right and freedom of the data subject.

260. Besides the awareness necessary to the processing of sensitive personal data, processing agents should process children's data carefully because of the difference in the Brazilian data protection regime, especially when it comes to the necessity of the consent of one of its parents or legal guardian (the only exception to that comes when the processing agent needs to reach the children's parents or legal guardian).

261. In this way, agents of processing should adopt security, technical and administrative measures that are sufficiently capable of protecting personal data from unauthorized access and accidental or illegal situations of destruction, loss, alteration, communication or any form of improper or unlawful processing pursuant to Article 46 of the LGPD.

Part IV. Data Subject Rights

262. The Brazilian legal system has always provided individuals with a range of fundamental rights based on the Federal Constitution of 1988 (Article 5º), which ensures to Brazilians and foreigners residing in the country being ensured of inviolability of the right to life, liberty, equality, security and property.

263. Consequently, the Brazilian Data Protection Act—also called LGPD—could not be different. Based on Europe's GDPR, the LGPD provides an arrangement of rights in its third chapter, mainly to provide data subjects its informational self-determination, which is one of the foundations of LGPD (Article 2º, II).

264. It consists of a right of the data subject, which gives him or her the power of decision over his or her own personal data; in other words, it provides the individual guarantee of freedom of decision regarding actions to be taken or omitted and even the possibility of behaving in accordance with such decision.[63]

265. Therefore, to ensure that the data subject will self-determinate regarding its personal data, the LGPD assured rights and, consequently, obligations to processing agents.

266. Starting in Article 17, the LGPD states that "every natural person is assured ownership of his or her personal data, with the fundamental rights of freedom, intimacy and privacy being guaranteed." These rights encompass the following:

1. **Right to be informed:** Article 9 and Article 18, items I, VII and VIII of LGPD
2. **Right of access:** Article 18, items I and II and Article 19 of LGPD
3. **Right of rectification:** Article 18, item III and §6 of LGPD
4. **Right to erasure:** Article 18, items IV, VI and §6 of LGPD
5. **Right to data portability:** Article 18, item V and §7 of LGPD
6. **Right to revocation of consent:** Article 18, item IX, and Article 8, §5 of LGPD
7. **Right to object:** Article 18, §2 of LGPD

63. Jürgen Schwabe, *50 Years of Case-Law of the German Federal Constitutional Court* 237 (trans. Beatriz Hennig et al., Fundacion Konrad-Adenauer 2005), Disponível em: http://www.kas.de/wf/doc/kas_7738-544-1- 30.pdf. Access on Apr. 11, 2020.

8. **Right to review decisions made solely based on automated processing:** Article 20 of LGPD

267. Even though Article 18 attributes the obligation to attend data subject rights to controllers, there is no barrier that prevents the data subject from trying to obtain the information from the processor too. Indeed, the third paragraph of this article stipulates that the rights shall be exercised by means of an express request to the processing agent, which can be either a Controller or a Processor. Notwithstanding, the LGPD stipulates the right to petition against the controller before the national authority (ANPD), which will be presented in the following chapters, and consumer protection bodies (when it is feasible).

268. Furthermore, the request as mentioned shall be fulfilled without costs to the data subject within the time periods and the terms as provided in the regulation. This means that nowadays, there is no deadline set for a controller to fulfill their obligations, with the exception of the rights to confirm the existence of or access to personal data, for which LGPD stipulates two deadlines to controllers in Article 19: (i) in a simplified format, immediately; or (ii) by means of a clear and complete declaration that indicates the origin of the data, the nonexistence of registration, the criteria used and the purpose of the processing, subject to commercial and industrial secrecy, provided within a period of fifteen days as from the date of the data subject's request.

269. Moreover, it is necessary to mention that public authorities have a different period to attend to the data subject's rights requests. According to Article 23 of LGPD, the time periods and procedures shall obey the provisions of specific legislation, especially the provisions stated in the Brazilian Habeas Data Law (Law No. 9,507/97), the Federal Administrative Procedure Law (Law No. 9,784/99) and the Brazilian Access to Information Law (Law No. 12,527/11).

270. Finally, it is important to state that beyond the administrative jurisdiction, the defense of the interests and rights of data subjects may be carried out in court, individually or collectively, as provided in pertinent legislation regarding the instruments of individual and collective protection (Article 22).

271. Hence, the Brazilian legal system offers a strong mechanism of rights and guarantees to data subjects. In the next chapters, these rights will be explained individually.

Chapter 1. Right to Be Informed

272. The right to be informed and the right to access are connected to the GDPR and, especially, in the LGPD. Different from the GDPR, which states many obligations to controllers with the duty to inform the data subject of a list of contents divided between the situation where personal data are collected from the data subject (Article 13, GDPR) and where personal data have not been obtained from the data subject (Article 14, GDPR), the LGPD is simpler.

273. The right to be informed is stated in Article 9 of LGPD, which has the following drafting:

> Article 9. The data subject has the right to facilitated access to information concerning the processing of his or her data, which must be made available in a clear, adequate, and ostensible manner, concerning, among other characteristics provided in regulation for complying with the principle of free access:
>
> I — the specific purpose of the processing;
> II — the type and duration of the processing, being observed commercial and industrial secrecy;
> III — identification of the controller;
> IV — the controller's contact information;
> V — information regarding the shared use of data by the controller and the purpose;
> VI — responsibilities of the agents that will carry out the processing; and
> VII — the data subject's rights, with explicit mention of the rights provided in Art. 18 of this Law.

274. Therefore, the LGPD states that the data subject has the right to be informed about the third parties that personal data is being shared (Articles 9, V and 18, VII), the contact details of the controller (Article 9, IV), the data subjects rights (Article 9, VII), the confirmation of the existence of the processing (Article 18, I) and if the processing of personal data is a condition for the provision of a product or service or for the exercise of a right, a situation which the data subject shall be informed with special highlight of this fact and by which means he or she may exercise his or her rights (Article 9, §3º).

275. Notwithstanding, the act brings information duties regarding the legal basis of consent. The controller shall inform the data subject of the possibility of denying consent and the consequences of such denial (Article 18, VIII). It is also important to state that the consent will be considered void if the information provided to the data subject contains misleading or abusive content or was not previously presented in a transparent, clear, and unambiguous way, in accordance with the first paragraph of the Article 9 of LGPD.

276. In addition, if there are changes in the purpose of the processing of personal data that are not compatible with the original consent, the controller shall previously inform the data subject of the changes of purpose, and the data subject may revoke his or her consent if he or she disagrees with the changes (§2º, Article 9).

277. It can be said that the right to information permeates all the other rights considering its nature to provide transparency to the data subject, especially about his or her rights.

278. In order to provide a better understanding of this right and the other data subject rights, a comparative table between the GDPR and the LGPD was elaborated, which will be presented at the end of each chapter:

RIGHT TO BE INFORMED	
LGPD	**GDPR**
Article **9.** The data subject has the right to facilitated access to information concerning the processing of his or her data, which much be made available in a clear, adequate and ostensible manner, concerning, among other characteristics provided in regulation for complying with the principle of free access: I — the specific purpose of the processing; II — the type and duration of the processing, being observed commercial and industrial secrecy; III — identification of the controller; IV — the controller's contact information; V — information regarding the shared use of data by the controller and the purpose; VI — responsibilities of the agents that will carry out the processing; and VII — the data subject's rights, with explicit mention of the rights provided in Article 18 of this Law.	1. Where personal data relating to a data subject are collected from the data subject, the controller shall, at the time when personal data are obtained, provide the data subject with all of the following information: (a) the identity and contact details of the controller and, where applicable, of the controller's representative; (b) the contact details of the data protection officer, where applicable; (c) the purposes of the processing for which the personal data are intended as well as the legal basis for the processing; (d) where the processing is based on point (f) of Article 6(1), the legitimate interests pursued by the controller or by a third party; (e) the recipients or categories of recipients of the personal data, if any;

RIGHT TO BE INFORMED	
LGPD	GDPR
§1 In situations where consent is required, it shall be considered void if the information provided to the data subject contains misleading or abusive content or was not previously presented in a transparent, clear and unambiguous way. §2 In the situation when consent is required, if there are changes in the purpose of the processing of personal data that are not compatible with the original consent, the controller shall previously inform the data subject of the changes of purpose, and the data subject may revoke his or her consent if she/he disagrees with the changes. §3 When the processing of personal data is a condition for the provision of a product or service or for the exercise of a right, the data subject shall be informed with special highlight of this fact and of the means by which she/he may exercise his or her data subject's rights as listed in Article 18 of this Law. Article 18. The data subject, regarding the data subject's data being processed by the controller, at any time and by means of request, has the right to obtain the following from the controller: I — confirmation of the existence of the processing; [...] VII — information about public and private entities with which the controller has shared data; VIII — information about the possibility of denying consent and the consequences of such denial; [...]	

RIGHT TO BE INFORMED	
LGPD	**GDPR**
	(f) where applicable, the fact that the controller intends to transfer personal data to a third country or international organization and the existence or absence of an adequacy decision by the Commission, or in the case of transfers referred to in Article 46 or 47, or the second subparagraph of Article 49(1), reference to the appropriate or suitable safeguards and the means by which to obtain a copy of them or where they have been made available. 2. In addition to the information referred to in paragraph 1, the controller shall, at the time when personal data are obtained, provide the data subject with the following further information necessary to ensure fair and transparent processing: (a) the period for which the personal data will be stored, or if that is not possible, the criteria used to determine that period; (b) the existence of the right to request from the controller access to and rectification or erasure of personal data or restriction of processing concerning the data subject or to object to processing, as well as the right to data portability; (c) where the processing is based on point (a) of Article 6(1) or point (a) of Article 9(2), the existence of the right to withdraw consent at any time

RIGHT TO BE INFORMED	
LGPD	GDPR
	without affecting the lawfulness of processing based on consent before its withdrawal; (d) the right to lodge a complaint with a supervisory authority; (e) whether the provision of personal data is a statutory or contractual requirement, or a requirement necessary to enter into a contract, as well as whether the data subject is obliged to provide the personal data and of the possible consequences of failure to provide such data; (f) the existence of automated decision-making, including profiling, referred to in Article 22(1) and (4) and, at least in those cases, meaningful information about the logic involved, as well as the significance and the envisaged consequences of such processing for the data subject. [...] **Article 14—Information to be provided where personal data have not been obtained from the data subject** 1. Where personal data have not been obtained from the data subject, the controller shall provide the data subject with the following information: (a) the identity and contact details of the controller and, where applicable, of the controller's representative;

RIGHT TO BE INFORMED	
LGPD	GDPR
	(b) the contact details of the data protection officer, where applicable; (c) the purposes of the processing for which the personal data are intended as well as the legal basis for the processing; (d) the categories of personal data concerned; (e) the recipients or categories of recipients of the personal data, if any; (f) where applicable, that the controller intends to transfer personal data to a recipient in a third country or international organization and the existence or absence of an adequacy decision by the Commission, or in the case of transfers referred to in Article 46 or 47, or the second subparagraph of Article 49(1), reference to the appropriate or suitable safeguards and the means to obtain a copy of them or where they have been made available. 2. In addition to the information referred to in paragraph 1, the controller shall provide the data subject with the following information necessary to ensure fair and transparent processing in respect of the data subject: (a) the period for which the personal data will be stored, or if that is not possible, the criteria used to determine that period; (b) where the processing is based on point (f) of Article 6(1), the legitimate interests pursued by the controller or by a third party;

RIGHT TO BE INFORMED	
LGPD	**GDPR**
	(c) the existence of the right to request from the controller access to and rectification or erasure of personal data or restriction of processing concerning the data subject and to object to processing, as well as the right to data portability; (d) where processing is based on point (a) of Article 6(1) or point (a) of Article 9(2), the existence of the right to withdraw consent at any time, without affecting the lawfulness of processing based on consent before its withdrawal; (e) the right to lodge a complaint with a supervisory authority; (f) from which source the personal data originate, and if applicable, whether it came from publicly accessible sources; (g) the existence of automated decision-making, including profiling, referred to in Article 22(1) and (4) and, at least in those cases, meaningful information about the logic involved, as well as the significance and the envisaged consequences of such processing for the data subject. [...]

Chapter 2. Right of Access

279. As mentioned, the right to information and the right to access are connected both in the GDPR and LGPD. Regarding the right of access, the LGPD states in Article 18, II that the data subject, at any time and by means of request, has the right to obtain from the controller access to the data.

280. This right formalizes the principle of free access, stated in item IV of Article 6 (LGPD), which guarantees to the data subjects facilitated and free-of-charge consultation about the form and duration of the processing, as well as about the integrity of their personal data.

281. The access to the personal data that is being processed by the controller is regulated by Article 9, as mentioned, which gives the obligation to the controller to provide: (i) specific purpose of the processing; (ii) type and duration of the processing; (iii) identification and contact details of the controller; (iv) information regarding the shared use of data by the controller and the purpose; (v) responsibilities of the agents that will carry out the processing; and (vi) data subject's rights.

282. Moreover, if the process originated from the consent of the data subject or from a contract, the data subject could request a complete electronic copy of his or her personal data, subject to commercial and industrial secrecy, in accordance with regulations of the national authority, in a format that allows its subsequent use, including to other processing operations, accordingly to the third paragraph of Article 19.

283. Furthermore, as mentioned before, the term to comply with the data subject's access request is regulated by Article 19, which states that the confirmation of the existence of or access to personal data shall be provided immediately, in a simplified format or within fifteen days from the date of the data subject's request by means of a clear and complete declaration that indicates the origin of the data, the nonexistence of registration, the criteria used and the purpose of the processing, subject to commercial and industrial secrecy.

284. It is important to note that the ANPD can provide different time periods for specific sectors. However, so far, there has been no regulation about the theme.

285. In addition, the personal data shall be stored in a format that facilitates the exercise of the right to access (Article 19, §1°) and provided by electronic means that is safe and suitable for this purpose or in printed form at the data subject's discretion (Article 19, §2°):

RIGHT OF ACCESS

LGPD	GDPR
Article 18. The data subject, regarding the data subject's data being processed by the controller, at any time and by means of request, has the right to obtain the following from the controller: I — confirmation of the existence of the processing; II — access to the data; [...] Article 19. Confirmation of the existence of or access to personal data shall be provided by means of request by the data subject: I — in a simplified format, immediately; or II — by means of a clear and complete declaration that indicates the origin of the data, the nonexistence of registration, the criteria used and the purpose of the processing, subject to commercial and industrial secrecy provided within a period of fifteen (15) days from the date of the data subject's request. §1 Personal data shall be stored in a format that facilitates the exercise of the right to access.	**Article 15—Right of access by the data subject** 1. The data subject shall have the right to obtain from the controller confirmation as to whether or not personal data concerning him or her are being processed and, where that is the case, access to the personal data and the following information: (a) the purposes of the processing; (b) the categories of personal data concerned; (c) the recipients or categories of recipients to whom the personal data have been or will be disclosed, in particular recipients in third countries or international organisations; (d) where possible, the envisaged period for which the personal data will be stored, or, if not possible, the criteria used to determine that period; (e) the existence of the right to request from the controller rectification or erasure of personal data or restriction of processing of personal data concerning the data subject or to object to such processing; (f) the right to lodge a complaint with a supervisory authority; (g) where the personal data are not collected from the data subject, any available information as to their source; (h) the existence of automated decision-making, including profiling, referred to in Article 22(1) and (4) and, at least in those cases, meaningful information about the logic

RIGHT OF ACCESS	
LGPD	**GDPR**
§2 Information and the data may be provided at the data subject's discretion: I — by electronic means that is safe and suitable for this purpose; or II — in printed form. §3 When processing originates from the consent of the data subject or from a contract, the data subject may request a complete electronic copy of his or her personal data, subject to commercial and industrial secrecy, in accordance with regulations of the national authority, in a format that allows its subsequent use, including for other processing operations. §4 The national authority may provide differently regarding the time periods provided in items I and II of the lead sentence of this article for specific sectors.	involved, as well as the significance and the envisaged consequences of such processing for the data subject. 2. Where personal data are transferred to a third country or to an international organization, the data subject shall have the right to be informed of the appropriate safeguards pursuant to Article 46 relating to the transfer. 3. The controller shall provide a copy of the personal data undergoing processing. For any further copies requested by the data subject, the controller may charge a reasonable fee based on administrative costs. Where the data subject makes the request by electronic means, and unless otherwise requested by the data subject, the information shall be provided in a commonly used electronic form. 4. The right to obtain a copy referred to in paragraph 3 shall not adversely affect the rights and freedoms of others.

Chapter 3. Right of Rectification

286. The right of rectification is linked to the data quality principle laid down the Article 6, item V of the LGPD, which guarantees to the data subjects the accuracy, clarity, relevancy and updating of the data in accordance with the need for achieving the purpose of the processing.

287. According to item III of Article 18, the data subject has the right to correct incomplete, inaccurate, or out-of-date data. Examples of rectification include requests to correct the spelling of a name or surname, date of birth, address, and the update of an email address, among others.

288. Furthermore, the controller shall immediately inform the processing agents with which he or she has carried out the shared use of data of the correction so that they can repeat an identical procedure, except in cases in which this action is proven impossible or involves disproportionate effort (Article 18, §6 of the LGPD).

289. It is important to mention that this right is also guaranteed by other means in the Brazilian legal system as in the context of the consumer relation, the Consumer's Rights Act (CDC) established by Law No. 8.078/90, which also gives to the consumer (data subject) the right to correction of his or her data and files that are inaccurate (Article 43, third paragraph).

290. In order to efficiently and promptly respond to the subjects' requests, preventing major damages from reaching them, it is crucial that the controller develop a privacy portal or any other means which enable people to easily report a possible failure or inadequacy with their own data that is being used by the company.

291. Tools such as the ones mentioned above are a central part of the privacy and data protection governance structure of each and every company, especially because it deals directly with the subjects that are the most important actors within a great part of the privacy-related strategies.

292. The rectification rights are meant to be quickly responded to, that is why normally it is expected that for such requests, the company answers the subjects immediately, at least in a simplified way, so they have a clear and first notion about how their data is being processed by the company.

293. Finally, it should be noted that the right of rectification is also provided in the GDPR:

RIGHT OF RECTIFICATION	
LGPD	**GDPR**
Article 18. The data subject, regarding the data subject's data being processed by the controller, at any time and by means of request, has the right to obtain the following from the controller: [...] III — correction of incomplete, inaccurate, or out-of-date data. [...] §6 The controller shall immediately inform the processing agents with which she/he has carried out the shared use of data of the correction, deletion, anonymization or blocking of data, so that they can repeat an identical procedure, except in cases in which this action is proven impossible or involves disproportionate effort.	Article 16—Right to rectification The data subject shall have the right to obtain from the controller without undue delay the rectification of inaccurate personal data concerning him or her. Considering the purposes of the processing, the data subject shall have the right to have incomplete personal data completed, including by means of providing a supplementary statement.

Chapter 4. Right to Erasure

294. The right to erasure is stated in the LGPD by items IV and VI of Article 18. Item IV specifies that the data subject can actually choose between the anonymization, blocking or deletion of personal data that are unnecessary, excessive or processed in noncompliance with the provisions of the Law.

295. In addition, item VI states that the data subjects can request from the controller the deletion of personal data processed with the consent unless one of the following situations applies: (i) the data are necessary to comply with a legal or regulatory obligation by the controller; (ii) the data are being used to conduct a study by a research entity; (iii) the data can/will be transferred to third parties, provided that the requirements for data processing as provided in this Law are obeyed; or (iv) the situation where data has been anonymized and are exclusively used by the controller, with no permitted access by third parties.

296. Furthermore, the controller shall immediately inform the processing agents with which he or she has carried out the shared use of data of the deletion, anonymization or blocking of data, so that they can repeat an identical procedure, except in cases in which this action is proven impossible or involves disproportionate effort (Article 18, §6 of the LGPD).

297. This right emerges very clearly from the exercise of informational self-determination that consists of the power of decision of the data subject over his or her own personal data.

298. At this point, it is important to mention that when the GDPR regulates the right to erasure, it also regulates the right to be forgotten. However, in the Brazilian legal system, although there is some discussion about the subject, the Federal Supreme Court, in the trial of Extraordinary Appeal (RE) No. 1010606, ruled that the right to be forgotten:

299. The idea of the right to be forgotten is incompatible with the Federal Constitution, understood as the power to prevent, due to the passage of time, the disclosure of facts or data truthfully and lawfully obtained and published in the media—analog or digital. Possible excesses or abuses in the exercise of freedom of expression and information must be analyzed on a case-by-case basis, based on constitutional parameters, especially those related to the protection of honor, image, privacy and personality in general, and the express and specific legal provisions in the criminal and civil spheres.[64]

300. Therefore, even if the data subject has the right to erasure and have his or her honor, image, privacy, and personality protected, he or she will not always have

64. Brazil, Federal Supreme Court. 2021. https://portal.stf.jus.br/noticias/verNoticiaDetalhe.asp?idConteudo=460414&ori=1.

the right to be forgotten. It would be analyzed case by case by the Brazilian judiciary.

RIGHT TO ERASURE	
LGPD	**GDPR**
Article 18. The data subject, regarding the data subject's data being processed by the controller, at any time and by means of request, has the right to obtain the following from the controller: [...] IV–anonymization, blocking or deletion of unnecessary or excessive data or data processed in noncompliance with the provisions of this Law; [...] VI–deletion of personal data processed with the consent of the data subject, except in the situations provided in Article 16 of this Law; [...] §6 The controller shall immediately inform the processing agents with which she/he has carried out the shared use of data of the correction, deletion, anonymization or blocking of data, so that they can repeat an identical procedure, except in cases in which this action is proven impossible or involves disproportionate effort.	Article 17—Right to erasure ('right to be forgotten') 1. The data subject shall have the right to obtain from the controller the erasure of personal data concerning him or her without undue delay and the controller shall have the obligation to erase personal data without undue delay where one of the following grounds applies: (a) the personal data are no longer necessary in relation to the purposes for which they were collected or otherwise processed; (b) the data subject withdraws consent on which the processing is based according to point (a) of Article 6(1), or point (a) of Article 9(2), and where there is no other legal ground for the processing; (c) the data subject objects to the processing pursuant to Article 21(1) and there are no overriding legitimate grounds for the processing, or the data subject objects to the processing pursuant to Article 21(2); (d) the personal data have been unlawfully processed; (e) the personal data have to be erased for compliance with a legal obligation in Union or Member State law to which the controller is subject; (f) the personal data have been collected in relation to the offer of information society services referred to in Article 8(1).

RIGHT TO ERASURE	
LGPD	**GDPR**
	2. Where the controller has made the personal data public and is obliged pursuant to paragraph 1 to erase the personal data, the controller, taking account of available technology and the cost of implementation, shall take reasonable steps, including technical measures, to inform controllers which are processing the personal data that the data subject has requested the erasure by such controllers of any links to, or copy or replication of, those personal data. [...]

Chapter 5. Right to Data Portability

301. As stated in item V of Article 18 of the LGPD, the data subject has the right to obtain the following from the controller the portability of the data to another service provider or product provider by means of an express request, pursuant to the regulations of the national authority, and subject to commercial and industrial secrets.

302. This is an important right due to the facilities it brings to the data subjects' lives. Differently from the GDPR, which states that data portability can only be performed if the processing is based on consent or on a contract and carried out by automated means, the only exception that the LGPD brings is that data portability does not include data that have already been anonymized by the controller.

303. An important aspect that has to be considered when relating to the right to data portability is the interoperability of the data. The portability necessarily involves a data transfer that has to be made in such a way that the data can be completely used by the company that receives it in order to guarantee the quality and integrity of the subject's data.

304. Interoperability is a must-have in every situation of data portability, and its importance can be observed in practice, especially in the discussions concerning the open banking strategy in Brazil. In such context, interoperability is crucial to make possible the exchange of the information necessary for data portability and also to enable the exchange of space for the effective sharing of integrated services.[65]

305. Although this right is stated in the LGPD, its exercise, conditions, terms and deadlines have not yet been regulated by the ANPD.

RIGHT TO DATA PORTABILITY	
LGPD	**GDPR**
Article 18. The data subject, regarding the data subject's data being processed by the controller, at any time and by means of request, has the right to obtain the following from the controller: [...]	Article 20—Right to data portability 1. The data subject shall have the right to receive the personal data concerning him or her, which he or she has provided to a controller, in a structured, commonly used and machine-readable format and have the right to transmit those data to another

65. Mario Viola & Patrícia Thomazelli, *Portabilidade de Dados, Interoperabilidade e Open Banking* (ITS-Rio 2021). Disponível em: https://itsrio.org/wp-content/uploads/2021/02/Portabilidade-Interoperabilidade-OpenBanking.pdf. Access on Dec. 2, 2022.

RIGHT TO DATA PORTABILITY	
LGPD	**GDPR**
V—portability of the data to another service provider or product provider, by the means of an express request, pursuant with the regulations of the national authority, and subject to commercial and industrial secrets; [...] §7 The portability of personal data referred to in item V of the lead sentence of this article does not include data that have already been anonymized by the controller.	controller without hindrance from the controller to which the personal data have been provided, where: (a) the processing is based on consent pursuant to point (a) of Article 6(1) or point (a) of Article 9(2) or on a contract pursuant to point (b) of Article 6(1); and (b) the processing is carried out by automated means. 2. In exercising his or her right to data portability pursuant to paragraph 1, the data subject shall have the right to have the personal data transmitted directly from one controller to another, where technically feasible. 3. The exercise of the right referred to in paragraph 1 of this Article shall be without prejudice to Article 17. That right shall not apply to processing necessary for the performance of a task carried out in the public interest or in the exercise of official authority vested in the controller. 4. The right referred to in paragraph 1 shall not adversely affect the rights and freedoms of others.

Chapter 6. Right to Revocation of Consent

306. Consent is one of the lawful grounds that allows controllers to process personal data. Although it is stated as the first legal basis in Articles 7 and 11, consent is not the only valid legal basis to process personal data.

307. In fact, consent is a delicate legal basis due to the many legal requirements, as already mentioned in Part II of this book. Besides its requirements of free, informed, and unambiguous manifestation by the data subject, where he or she agrees to his or her processing of personal data for a given purpose, consent can be revoked at any time, in accordance with item IX of the Article 18 of LGPD.

308. To revoke the consent, the data subject should make an express request through a facilitated and free-of-charge procedure. Nevertheless, it is emphasized that the processing carried out under prior consent will remain valid as long as there is no request for elimination, in terms of point VI of the main sentence of Article 18 of the Law.

309. Because of the possibility of revoking the consent for the processing, this legal basis is really fragile for the controllers since, at any time, the subjects can request the processing to be stopped. If such situation occurs, the data controller has no other option besides proceeding as demanded by the individual.

310. That is why it normally is advised that before opting for consent as the legal basis for the processing activities, the controllers should observe whether the other options of applicable legal basis could also justify the processing so as to give greater legal certainty for the controller's actions.

RIGHT TO REVOCATION OF CONSENT	
LGPD	**GDPR**
Article 18. The data subject, regarding the data subject's data being processed by the controller, at any time and by means of request, has the right to obtain the following from the controller: [...] IX—revocation of consent as provided in §5 of Article 8 of this Law.	Article 7.3—Conditions for consent 3. The data subject shall have the right to withdraw his or her consent at any time. The withdrawal of consent shall not affect the lawfulness of processing based on consent before its withdrawal. Prior to giving consent, the data subject shall be informed thereof. It shall be as easy to withdraw as to give consent.

RIGHT TO REVOCATION OF CONSENT	
LGPD	**GDPR**
Article 8 The consent provided in item I of Article 7 of this Law shall be given in writing or by other means able to demonstrate the manifestation of the will of the data subject. [...] §5 Consent may be revoked at any time, by express request of the data subject, through a facilitated and free of charge procedure, with processing carried out under previously given consent remaining valid as long as there is no request for deletion, pursuant to item VI of the lead sentence of Article 18 of this Law.	

Chapter 7. Right to Object

311. Unlike the European regulation (GDPR), which brings clear situations in which the data subject can object to the processing of his or her personal data as situations in which the legal basis is legitimate interest or public interest, as well as situations of direct marketing and profiling, the LGPD does not bring clear provisions regarding the exercise of this right.

312. In accordance with Article 18, paragraph 2 of LGPD, the data subject may object to the processing carried out based on one of the situations of waiver of consent if there is noncompliance with the provisions of this Law.

313. With this provision, it is understood that the data subject has the right to object to the processing of personal data when it is based on items II to X of Article 7 of LGPD or on any of the subparagraphs of item II of Article 11.

314. However, the exercise of this right is not explicit in the LGPD; there are no clear provisions about the situations in which the data subject can object to the processing of his or her personal data, how the controller must attend to this right and how its process would be handled inside of the organization. There is a need for regulation in this regard by the ANPD, in particular, to provide guidance on the situations in which the controller must stop processing personal data and the situations in which it may retain them.

315. It is believed that, in this situation, the controller must be able to demonstrate on which legal basis the data flow is based. Normally, there are situations that the controller can keep the processing of personal data, e.g., to comply with legal obligations or for the regular exercise of rights in judicial, administrative or arbitration procedures. However, only with the ANPD's guidance the exercise of this right will be demystified:

RIGHT TO OBJECT	
LGPD	**GDPR**
Article 18. The data subject, regarding the data subject's data being processed by the controller, at any time and by means of request, has the right to obtain the following from the controller: [...]	Article 21—Right to object 1. The data subject shall have the right to object, on grounds relating to his or her particular situation, at any time to processing of personal data concerning him or her which is based on point (e) or (f) of Article 6(1), including profiling based on those provisions.

RIGHT TO OBJECT	
LGPD	**GDPR**
§2 The data subject may object the processing carried out based on one of the situations of waiver of consent, if there is noncompliance with the provisions of this Law.	The controller shall no longer process the personal data unless the controller demonstrates compelling legitimate grounds for the processing which override the interests, rights and freedoms of the data subject or for the establishment, exercise or defense of legal claims. 2. Where personal data are processed for direct marketing purposes, the data subject shall have the right to object at any time to processing of personal data concerning him or her for such marketing, which includes profiling to the extent that it is related to such direct marketing. 3. Where the data subject objects to processing for direct marketing purposes, the personal data shall no longer be processed for such purposes. 4. At the latest at the time of the first communication with the data subject, the right referred to in paragraphs 1 and 2 shall be explicitly brought to the attention of the data subject and shall be presented clearly and separately from any other information. [...]

Chapter 8. Right to Review Decisions Made Solely Based on Automated Processing

316. According to the Article 20 of the LGPD, the data subject has the right to request the review of decisions made solely based on automated processing of personal data affecting his or her interests, including decisions intended to define his or her personal, professional, consumer and credit profile, or aspects of his or her personality.

317. It is important to mention that not all automated processing is subject to this right, only those based exclusively on automated processing which influence the rights and freedoms of the data subject, such as profiling.

318. Decisions taken exclusively by automated decision-making are those in which there is no human interference. Therefore, in a situation where there is a chatbot that has artificial intelligence that performs the first attendance of the data subject, collects his or her personal data and forwards him or her to an attendant who analyzes and solves his or her problem, the data subject has no right to request a review about it.

319. Nonetheless, in case the chatbot, using artificial intelligence, collects the personal data of the data subject, analyzes it, and decides on its own (e.g., credit application analysis), there is a situation where the decision was made solely based on automated processing, and the data subject may request its review.

320. In situations where the data subject exercises its rights, the controller shall provide clear and adequate information regarding the criteria and procedures used for an automated decision, subject to commercial and industrial secrecy, in accordance with the first paragraph of Article 20. And if there is no offer of information based on commercial and industrial secrecy, the national authority may carry out an audit to verify discriminatory aspects in automated processing of personal data.

321. This is one of the data subject's rights that the Brazilian judicial system should be aware of. There is much artificial intelligence being used to support the decisions of higher courts, such as VICTOR, the artificial intelligence system of the Supreme Federal Court (STF). If in a newer future, the AI effectively begins to decide court cases on its own, the judiciary will likely need to maintain a mechanism that allows this review requests to the data subject, as well as establish procedures so that it can comply with these requests in accordance with the LGPD:

RIGHT TO REVIEW DECISIONS MADE SOLELY BASED ON AUTOMATED PROCESSING	
LGPD	**GDPR**
Article 20. The data subject has the right to request for the review of decisions made solely based on automated processing of personal data affecting his or her interests, including decisions intended to define his or her personal, professional, consumer and credit profile, or aspects of his or her personality. §1 Whenever requested to do so, the controller shall provide clear and adequate information regarding the criteria and procedures used for an automated decision, subject to commercial and industrial secrecy. §2 If there is no offer of information as provided in §1 of this article, based on commercial and industrial secrecy, the national authority may carry out an audit to verify discriminatory aspects in automated processing of personal data.	Article 22—Automated individual decision-making, including profiling 1. The data subject shall have the right not to be subject to a decision based solely on automated processing, including profiling, which produces legal effects concerning him or her or similarly significantly affects him or her. 2. Paragraph 1 shall not apply if the decision: (a) is necessary for entering into, or performance of, a contract between the data subject and a data controller; (b) is authorised by Union or Member State law to which the controller is subject and which also lays down suitable measures to safeguard the data subject's rights and freedoms and legitimate interests; or (c) is based on the data subject's explicit consent. 3. In the cases referred to in points (a) and (c) of paragraph 2, the data controller shall implement suitable measures to safeguard the data subject's rights and freedoms and legitimate interests, at least the right to obtain human intervention on the part of the controller, to express his or her point of view and to contest the decision. 4. Decisions referred to in paragraph 2 shall not be based on special categories of personal data referred to in Article 9(1), unless point (a) or (g) of Article 9(2) applies and suitable measures to safeguard the data subject's rights and freedoms and legitimate interests are in place.

Part V. Duties of Controllers and Processors

322. The topics covered in this Part V have excellent materials prepared by the ANPD. Considering the extensive level of clarifications, definitions and examples contained in the documents drawn up by the ANPD, free translations of them will be inserted below, as well as the articles of the General Personal Data Protection Law (LGPD) referred to in them.

323. According to its competences, the ANPD published, on May 28, 2021, its first guideline[66] to "establish non-binding guidelines for processing agents to explain who may exercise the function of controller, processor and DPO; the legal definitions; the respective regimes of responsibility; specific cases which exemplify the explanations of the ANPD and frequently asked questions on the subject."

324. To better understand the responsibilities assigned to each, the ANPD has as it follows who can be considered a processing agent:

> 1. PROCESSING AGENTS. Who can be considered a processing agent?
>
> 6. Processing agents are the controller and the processor which may be natural or legal persons, governed by public or private law. It should be emphasized that the processing agents must be defined on the basis of their institutional nature. Subordinate individuals, such as employees, public servants or work teams of an organization, are not considered controllers (autonomous or joint) or processors, as they act under the directive power of the processing agent.
> 67. In the context of a legal person, the organization is the processing agent for the purposes of the LGPD, as it is the organization that establishes the rules for the processing of personal data to be carried out by its representatives or agents.
> 8. But in addition, the processing agent is defined for each personal data processing operation, so the same organization may be both controller and processor, according to its actions in different processing operations.
> 9. As we shall see below, natural persons may be considered controllers or processors of personal data. They will be controllers when they act in accordance

66. Guia Orientativo para Definições dos Agentes de Tratamento de Dados Pessoais: https://www.gov.br/anpd/pt-br/documentos-e-publicacoes/2021.05.27GuiaAgentesdeTratamento_Final.pdf. Accessed on Nov. 16, 2021.

with their own interests, with power of decision over the purposes and essential elements of processing. They will be processors when they act in accordance with the interests of the controller, being allowed only to define elements that are not essential to the purpose of the processing. The processor should be an entity distinct from the controller, i.e. not acting as a professional subordinate to the controller or as a member of its bodies.

10. On the other hand, employees will act in subordination to the decisions of the controller, not to be confused, therefore, with personal data processors.

11. As an example, a company decides to send advertisements to its clients with the purpose of leveraging the sales of a certain product. For this purpose, it hires an advertising agency, which will prepare the marketing campaign with photos of people using the product. The company informs all the criteria for the campaign, such as the target audience and establishes the criteria for the physical appearance of the photographic models. The advertising agency handles personal data to provide the service for the company, by selecting photo models and storing their photos. After the service is completed by the agency, the company employee sends the advertisements to the customers.

12. In this example the company acts as controller, by determining the data processing and defining its essential elements. The advertising agency acts as processor by processing data according to the purpose of the processing defined by the controller. And the employee, when sending e-mails to clients, acts under the directive power of the company and is not characterized as a processing agent."

Chapter 1. National Rules Regarding Duties of Controllers

325. It is up to the controllers to demonstrate, through their own records and operators acting on their behalf and under their guidance, that it can maintain compliance with laws and regulations, maintaining the confidentiality and legitimate processing of data subject.

326. On this topic, the ANPD guideline provides:

> 2. CONTROLLER
>
> 2.1 Legal definition
>
> 13. The controller is the agent responsible for making the main decisions concerning the processing of personal data and for defining the purpose of this processing. These decisions include the instructions given to contracted processors to carry out a particular processing of personal data.
> 14. The legal definition of controller is found in Article 5, VI, of the LGPD:
>
> Natural or legal person, whether of public or private law, responsible for decisions regarding the processing of personal data.
>
> 15. The concept has high practical importance, since the LGPD attributes specific obligations to the controller, such as that of preparing a data protection impact report (Article 38[67]), that of proving that the consent obtained from the data subject meets the legal requirements (Article 8, § 2[68]) and that of communicating to the ANPD the occurrence of security incidents (Article 48[69]). In addition, the attribution of responsibilities regarding redress for damages arising from unlawful acts is distinct according to the qualification of the processing agent, i.e., if controller or processor, as provided in Articles 42 to 45.[70]

67 Article 38. The national authority may determine that the controller must draft a data protection impact report, including on sensitive data, referring to its data processing operations, pursuant the terms of regulation, observing commercial and industrial secrecy.

68. Article 8. The consent provided in item I of Art. 7 of this law shall be given in writing or by other means able to demonstrate the intention of the data subject. (…)

§2 The burden of proof to demonstrate that the consent was dully obtained in compliance with the provisions of this Law is on the controller.

69. Article 48. The controller must communicate to the national authority and to the data subject the occurrence of a security incident that may create risk or relevant damage to the data subjects.

70. Article 42. The controller or the processor are both responsible for the pecuniary, moral, individual or collective damage that has occurred due to its activity of processing personal data in violation of the national legislation. The processor shall be jointly and severally liable for the damage caused by the processing, whenever it has disobeyed the legislation or not followed the lawful instructions of the controller. Furthermore, the controller shall be jointly liable for the processing in which it was directly involved.

Art. 43. The processing agents shall not be held liable if they prove that: they have not carried out the personal data processing that is attributed to them; although they have carried out the processing of personal data that is attributed to them, there was no violation of the data protection legislation; the damage arises from the exclusive fault of the data subject or a third party.

16. It is also worth mentioning that the data subject's rights (Article 18[71]) are, as a rule, exercised against the controller, which is responsible for, among other measures, providing information regarding the processing, ensuring

---

Art. 44. The processing of personal data shall be considered as irregular when it fails to comply with the legislation or when it does not provide the security that the data subject can expect, considering the relevant circumstances of the processing, such as the way the processing was carried out, the result and the risks reasonably expect of it, and the techniques for processing personal data available at the time it was carried out.

Art. 45. In those cases which the violation of data subject's rights is in the scope of consumer relationship, the rules of liability provided in the pertinent legislation remains applicable.

71. Article 18. The data subject has the right to obtain from the controller, with regard to the data subject's data processed by it, at any time and upon request:

I — confirmation of the existence of the processing;
II — access to the data;
III — correction of incomplete, inaccurate or out-of-date data;
IV — anonymization, blocking or elimination of unnecessary or excessive data or data processed in violation of the provisions of this Law;
V — portability of data to another service or product provider, upon express request, in accordance with the regulations of the national authority, with due observance of commercial and industrial secrets;
VI — elimination of personal data processed with the consent of the data subject, except in the cases provided in Art. 16 of this law;
VII — information of public and private entities with which the controller has carried out shared use of the data;
VIII — information about the possibility of not providing consent and the consequences of such refuse;
IX — withdraw of consent as provided in §5 of art. 8 hereof.

§1 The personal data subject has the right to petition, regarding his data, against the controller before the national authority.

§2 The data subject may object the processing carried out on the basis of one of the cases of waiver of consent, in case of noncompliance with the provisions of this law.

§3 The rights provided in this article shall be exercised at the express request of the data subject or legally constituted representative, to the processing agent.

§4 In the event of impossibility for immediate adoption of the measure pursuant §3 of this article, the controller shall send a reply to the data subject in which may:

I — communicate that it is not the data processing agent and indicate, whenever possible, the agent; or
II — indicate the factual or legal reasons that prevent the immediate adoption of the measure.

§5 The request referred to in §3 of this article will be attended to without cost to the data subject, within the time limits and under the terms provided for in the regulations.

§6 The party responsible must immediately inform the processing agents with which has shared data of the correction, elimination, anonymization or blocking of data, in order to them repeat identical procedure, except in cases in which this action is proven impossible or involves disproportionate effort.

§7 The portability of personal data referred to in item V of the caput of this article does not include data that have already been anonymized by the controller.

§8 The right referred to in §1 of this article may also be exercised before consumer protection agencies.

the correction and elimination of personal data, and receiving requests objecting the processing. The data subject may also petition against the controller before ANPD, what denotes the relevance of understanding the concept not only for professionals in the area, but also for ordinary citizens.

17. The identification of the controller must be based on the legal concept and on the auxiliary parameters indicated in this Guide, always considering the factual context and the relevant circumstances of the case. The role of controller may expressly derive from obligations stipulated in legal and regulatory instruments or in a contract signed between the parties. However, the actual activity performed by an organization may differ from what is established in the formal legal provisions, which is why it is of utmost importance to assess whether the alleged controller is in fact the one responsible for the main decisions regarding the processing.

2.2 Legal Person Controller

18. In most cases, the controller will be a legal person, whether governed by private or public law. This is what happens, for example, when companies or public entities make the main decisions regarding the storage, elimination or sharing of information that integrate a personal database managed within the organization.
According to the Civil Code, legal person governed by private law may be:
(a) nonprofit entities, such as associations, foundations, religious organizations, trade unions and political parties; or
(b) for-profit entities, such as business or simple companies, cooperatives and the EIRELI (Limited Liability Sole Proprietorship). Domestic public legal persons are the federated entities (Union, States, Federal District and Municipalities), in addition to public administration entities, such as municipalities and public foundations. Foreign states and international organisations are legal persons of external public law.
Therefore, all these entities may be considered as controllers for the purposes of the LGPD.

19. It follows that natural persons who act as professionals subordinate to a legal person or as members of its bodies are not controllers. This is the case of employees, administrators, partners, public servants and other natural persons that integrate the legal person and whose acts express their actions.

20. In this sense, the legal definition of controller must not be understood as a rule of internal distribution of powers and responsibilities. Rather, it is a legal command that assigns specific obligations to the legal person, so that assumes liability for the acts performed by its agents and representatives vis-à-vis the data subjects and the ANPD.

2.3 Controller legal person of public law

21. A peculiar situation is that of legal person of public law, whose decision powers are internally distributed among different public agencies. This is what takes place, for example, with the Union (legal person of public law)

and the Ministries (public agencies with no personality that are part of the Union and carry out personal data processing in accordance with the provisions of the legislation).

22. In these cases, two central aspects must be considered. On the one hand, according to Article 5, VI,[72] of the LGPD, the controller is the Union, a legal person of public law that is ultimately responsible for obligations arising from the law, contractual instruments or unlawful acts practiced by its bodies and public servants.
23. On the other hand, the LGPD has assigned to public bodies typical controller obligations, indicating that, in the public sector, these obligations must be distributed among the main depersonalized administrative units that integrate the legal person of public law and carry out personal data processing.
24. In this sense, the Union, as controller, is responsible before the LGPD, but the controller attributions, by virtue of administrative deconcentrating, are exercised by the public agencies performing functions on behalf of the legal person of which they are part, a phenomenon that characterizes the internal distribution of powers. This is what takes place in the hypotheses of shared use of personal data (Article 26[73]), meeting the requirements of the ANPD (Article 29[74]) and application of administrative sanctions (Article 52, § 3[75]).
25. In the same sense, it is emphasized that public bodies must comply with the duties of transparency and of appointing an officer (person named by the controller and processor to act as a communication channel between the controller, the data subjects and the ANPD), because in addition to acting on behalf of the legal person of which they are part, such obligations expressly arise from the LGPD (Article 23, I and III[76]).

---

72. Article 5. For purposes of this Law, it is considered:

    VI — controller: natural or legal person, whether of public or private law, responsible for decisions regarding the processing of personal data.

73. Article 26. The shared use of personal data by public authorities must meet the specific purposes of execution of public policies and legal attribution by the public agencies and entities, respecting the principles of personal data protection provided in art. 6 of this Law.
74. Article 29. The national authority may request, at any time, from agencies and entities of the Public Administration performing personal data processing operations, the specific information on the scope and nature of the data and other details of the processing performed and may issue a supplementary technical opinion to ensure compliance with this Law.
75. Article 52. Data processing agents, as a consequence of violations of the rules provided for in this law, shall be subject to the following administrative sanctions applicable by the national authority:

    §3 The provisions of items I, IV, V, VI, X, XI and XII of the caput of this article may be applied to agencies and public entities, without prejudice to the provisions of Law No. 8,112 of 11 December 1990, Law No. 8,429 of 2 June 1992 and Law No. 12,527 of 18 November 2011.

76. Article 23. The processing of personal data by legal entities of public law referred to in the sole paragraph of Art. 1 of Law No. 12,527, of Nov. 18, 2011 (Information Access Law), shall be carried out

26. Finally, it should be added that such bodies must establish adequate structures to receive requests from data subjects and requests for measures determined by the ANPD.
27. Consider the following example: in a contracting of a cloud computing solution from a company by a particular Ministry of the Executive Power, the controller is the Union, but it is the Ministry, as a federal public body, which will exercise the typical functions of the controller. In turn, the processor will be the contracted company. As it performs typical controller functions, it is up to the Ministry to appoint a data protection officer, as well as to make notifications to the ANPD in cases of security incidents, among other obligations set out in the LGPD. However, if a data subject decides to file a lawsuit challenging the processing performed, he or she must file against the controller, which is the Union.
28. In short, the attribution of specific legal obligations for public bodies arises from the complexity of administrative structures and their practical implications for the rights of data subjects, especially in view of the carrying out of data processing for different purposes by different bodies. Therefore, in addition to defining the legal person of public law as controller, the LGPD also assigned specific legal obligations for the various public bodies that carry out personal data processing.
29. Thus, in conclusion: in personal data processing operations conducted by public bodies that are depersonalized the legal person of public law to which the bodies are linked is the controller of personal data and therefore responsible for compliance with the LGPD.
30. However, due to the principle of administrative deconcentration, the depersonalized public body will perform typical functions of a data controller, in accordance with the obligations set out in the LGPD.
31. This conclusion refers only to the direct Public Administration, since the indirect administration follows the legal person regulation established by the LGPD.

2.4 Controller natural person

32. A natural person may be a controller in situations in which he/she is responsible for the main decisions regarding the processing of personal

---

to meet their public purpose, in pursuit of the public interest, for the purpose of performing legal capabilities or discharging legal attributions of the public interest, aiming to execute the legal powers or fulfilling the legal attributions of the public service, provided that:

> I — they inform the cases in which, in the exercise of their competences, they carry out the processing of personal data, providing clear and updated information on the legal provision, the purpose, the procedures and the practices used for the execution of these activities, in easily accessible means, preferably on their websites;
> II — (vetoed); and
> III — a data protection officer be appointed when carrying out personal data processing operations, pursuant to art. 39 of this Law.

data. In this hypothesis, the natural person acts independently and on its own behalf—and not in a subordinate manner to a legal person or as a member of a body thereof.

33. This is what takes place, for example, with sole proprietor, liberal professionals (such as lawyers, accountants and doctors) and those responsible for extra-judicial notaries.

2.5 Decisions of the controller

34. According to the provisions of the LGPD, the controller is responsible for making the "decisions regarding the processing of personal data" (Article 5, VI[77])
35. It is clear from this legal provision that the processing does not need to be carried out directly by the controller. Although the controller also processes personal data, the distinctive element is the power of decision, admitting that the controller provides instructions for a third party ("processor") to perform the processing on its behalf (Article 5, VII;[78] Article 39[79]).
36. The second relevant point is that it is not necessary that all decisions be made by the controller, being enough that he keeps under his influence and controls the main decisions, i.e., those related to the essential elements for the fulfillment of the purpose of the processing. In fact, especially when a processor is hired, it is usual and legitimate that part of the decisions regarding the processing, limited to its nonessential elements, remains under the authority of the processor. For example, the choice of software and equipment to be used and the details of prevention and security measures may be mentioned.
37. The third point to be considered is related to the definition of the decision-making elements that are characterized as "main" or "essential" and that, therefore, must remain under the control of the controller. Among these main decision-making elements, the definition of the purpose of the processing stands out, which will always be established by the controller, who is responsible, in accordance with the provisions of the LGPD, for stipulating the objectives that justify the processing, as well as its respective legal basis. Consider the following examples of decisions of the controller, according to the purpose of the processing: use of personal data to pay employees, conduct a customer survey, promote a marketing campaign, secure storage of information, or issue airline tickets.

---

77. *See* n. 7 on item n° 20.
78. Article 5. For purposes of this Law, it is considered:

    VII — processor: natural or legal person, whether of public or private law, which performs the processing of personal data on behalf of the controller.

79. Article 39. The processor shall carry out the processing in accordance with the instructions provided by the controller, which shall verify the compliance with their own instructions and with the rules on the matter.

38. Finally, in addition to the purpose, the controller is responsible for establishing other essential elements regarding the processing. This is the case of defining the nature of the personal data processed (for example, data of beneficiaries of a health plan or people registered in an official database) and the duration of the processing, i.e., the period during which the operation shall be carried out, including the establishment of a deadline for eliminate the data. It should be noted that other elements may be considered essential depending on the context and peculiarities of the specific case.

2.6 Examples

39. Following are some examples demonstrating who may assume the role of controller depending on the scenario.

Example 1—Self-employed doctor
A doctor, self-employed professional, stores the medical records and other personal data of her patients on the computer in her office. The doctor, who is a natural person, is the controller of the personal data.
Example 2—A doctor employed by a hospital
A doctor is an employee of a hospital, which is constituted as a non-profit-making association. In this capacity, she acts as the hospital's main representative vis-à-vis a cloud storage service for patient data, including by signing the corresponding contracts. The hospital, i.e., the civil association, legal person of private law, is the controller in this case. The doctor, as she acts under the directive power of the organization, is not characterized as a processing agent.
Example 3—Public agency contracting an artificial intelligence service
A public agency, bound to the Federal Government, hires an artificial intelligence solution provided by a company with the specific purpose of performing the automated processing of decisions based on a database managed by the agency. Following the instructions provided by the responsible public manager and established in the contract, the company performs the necessary operations to enable the processing of the data in question. The Union, a legal person of public law, is the controller in this case. Nevertheless, the responsible public body has specific legal obligations towards the data subjects and the ANPD, as provided in the LGPD. The company is the processor, since it performs the data processing according to the instructions provided by the controller. Finally, the public manager responsible, acting as a public servant subordinate to the Union, is not characterized as a processing agent.

327. It is crucial to have a clear understanding that the controller shall answer all the subject's requests, independent of its fault or direct relation to what was questioned. The controllers are the main ones responsible for anything related to the processing that has previously defined the means since it has the decision power over the whole activity. In cases where the processor has acted alone and disregarded the controller's determinations, the latest should answer the subjects, but it can demand the due responsibility for the processor in court, according to Article 42, § 4º of LGPD.

328. To clearly present to all stakeholders the compliance of the controller to the LGPD and the legitimacy of the processing activities led by it, the controller shall elaborate and constantly update the Record of Processing Activities (RoPA), as written in Article 37 of LGPD. This document is also important to prove the noninvolvement of the controller in processing activities that were misled by the processors.

Chapter 2. National Rules Regarding Joint Controllers

329. There is no provision for joint controllership in the LGPD; however, it is possible to identify situations in which the same operation involves more than one controller and involves common decisions or converging decisions of the purposes and essential elements for the processing of personal data.

330. It is important to understand that the mere fact of the presence of two processing agents participating in the same activity does not imply that there is a joint controller's case. To identify if a determined situation is indeed the case of joint controllership, two points shall be observed: the controllers must have the same objectives in the leading of the activity, and they also must consensually decide the means for the processing.

331. The LGPD, as already mentioned, has not a specific normative framework concerning how to determine the cases of joint controllership. Although, in Article 42, § 1°, the Law enlightens that the controller shall be jointly liable for the processing in which it was directly involved, presenting a first and basic idea of joint controllership.

332. According to the provisions of the ANPD below, such situations can be understood as joint controllership:

> 3. JOINT CONTROLLERSHIP AND SINGLE CONTROLLERSHIP
>
> 3.1 Difference—definition of purposes and essential elements together.
>
> 40. Depending on the context, the same personal data processing operation may involve more than one controller. According to the LGPD, Article 42, §1, II,[80] when more than one controller is directly involved in processing which results in damage to data subject, they will be jointly liable, except in the cases provided for in Article 43.[81]
> 41. Thus, although the LGPD does not spell out the concept of joint controller, it is possible to infer that it is contemplated in the data protection legal system. The definition of the functions of joint controllers entails consequences with regard to the functions of processing agents and the rights of data subjects.
> 42. Considering the inspiration of the LGPD in European law, it is possible to seek to in the latter norm, for clarification, for the definition of joint controllers (Article 26 of the GDPR):
>
> "Where two or more controllers jointly determine the purposes and means of processing, they shall be joint controllers. They shall in a transparent manner determine their respective responsibilities for compliance with the obligations under this Regulation, in particular as regards the exercising of the rights of

80. *See* n. 5 on item n° 14.
81. *See ibid.*

the data subject and their respective duties to provide the information referred to in Articles 13 and 14, by means of an arrangement between them unless, and in so far as, the respective responsibilities of the controllers are determined by Union or Member State law to which the controllers are subject. The arrangement may designate a contact point for data subjects."

43. For the European Regulation, joint controllership takes place when there is a "joint participation" in determining the "purposes and means of processing." According to the European Data Protection Board (EDPB), the purpose of the processing may arise from common or convergent decisions.
44. In joint decisions, two or more entities have a common intention on the purposes and means of processing and make decisions jointly. By contrast, in converging decisions there are distinct decisions being taken, but they complement each other in such a way that the processing would not be possible without the participation of both controllers.
45. However, even if the same set of data is processed, there will be no joint controllership if the processing objectives are different. For example, several controllers may process open government data, each one for their own specific purposes. If these purposes are not common, convergent or complementary, both will be singular controllers in relation to data processing and joint controllership will not be established, which would rule out the incidence of Article 42, §1, II,[82] of the LGPD.
46. As in the singular controller, joint controllers are able to determine the essential elements of the processing. This decision is made collectively, but there is no need for each controller to determine all the elements involved in a processing operation for joint controllership to be established.
47. It is important to emphasize, however, that the identification of joint controllership will be contextual and only the specific case will allow identifying in which cases the joint controllership was established. Once it is configured, the liability of the controllers will be joint and several, under the terms of Article 42, §1, II[83] which reinforces the importance of all being in compliance with the LGPD.
48. Thus, by adapting to the European conception to the LGPD scenario, the concept of joint controllers can be understood as "the joint, common or convergent determination, by two or more controllers, of the purposes and essential elements for carrying out the processing of personal data, by means of an agreement establishing their respective responsibilities regarding compliance with the LGPD."

3.2 How to assess if there is joint controllership

49. In summary, the existence of joint controller is verified when the following criteria are observed:
    1. More than one controller has decision-making power over the processing of personal data;

82. *See ibid.*
83. *See ibid.*

2. There is mutual interest of two or more controllers, based on their own purposes, over the same processing; and
3. Two or more controllers make common or converging decisions on the purposes and essential elements of the processing.

50. All the above criteria should be observed for the existence of joint controllership to be recognised.

3.3 Examples
Example 4—Use of open data made available by Regulatory Agency
The Regulatory Agency provides public access to data related to the granting of regulated services, including information about natural persons partners of service providers. The database is stored by the Agency itself and used to support administrative decisions. Civil Society Organisation has access to the data made available by the Agency and, based on artificial intelligence solution, cross-references with other databases in order to carry out social control actions of public entities and agents. The Business Company also handles the data in question, however, aiming to provide consulting services to the agents of the regulated sector.
Although the same database is used by the three entities (Regulatory Agency, Civil Society Organisation and Business Corporation), each one of these organisations is responsible and accountable for their respective processing. In this context, there is no joint controllership because the processing of data takes place within the scope of the activities and purposes defined by each organization.
Example 5—I-company marketing campaign: joint decisions
The companies ARGENTINA and BRASIL have launched a co-branded product COSMÉTICO and want to organize an event to promote this product. For this purpose, they decide to share data of their respective customers and database of potential customers and decide on the guest list for the event based on this data. They also agree on the modalities of sending the invitations to the event, how to collect feedback during the events and on the follow-up marketing actions. Finally, they hire the marketing agency DINAMARCA to execute the campaign. The agency brings suggestions on how customers could be better reached and defines the channels, tools and products of the campaign.
The companies ARGENTINA and BRASIL can be considered joint controllers for the processing of personal data in connection with the organization of the event and promotion of the COSMÉTICO brand product, as they have jointly defined the purpose and the essential elements of the data processed in this context.
The marketing agency DINAMARCA will act as data processor for the companies ARGENTINA and BRASIL. Although it has an opinion on the means of processing, it is not responsible for making the final decision, limiting itself to defining non-essential elements such as the channels, tools and products of the campaign.
If the marketing agency DINAMARCA hires third party cloud data storage services, e.g., this service provider will be characterised as a sub-processor.
Example 6—Company marketing campaign II: autonomous decisions

> Consider now that the campaign described in the previous example was so successful that, in a second moment, the company ARGENTINA hires the marketing agency DINAMARCA to advertise its products ESPELHO and FACA. A short time later, BRASIL takes the same decision to advertise its GARRAFA and HALTERE products. Both companies start using the list of clients they had previously shared.
> In this situation, which involves the advertising of products produced exclusively by company ARGENTINA or by company BRASIL, they will act as singular controllers, each acting in their own campaigns. The marketing agency DINAMARCA will continue as processor for each company.
> Example 7—Company marketing campaign III: holding company and subsidiary
> XRAY, a company that provides services through a digital platform, is headquartered in the United Kingdom. Due to the need of market its services and to gain more knowledge about the interests of the Brazilian public, it opens a subsidiary YANKEE in Brazil, which acts only according to its instructions.
> Despite being part of the same economic group, the holding company XRAY and the Brazilian subsidiary YANKEE have different legal personalities and, depending on the type of personal data processing operation and the circumstances of the specific case, they may act as controllers or processors, according to the specific case.
> In the processing of data for the marketing campaign conducted by the Brazilian subsidiary YANKEE, with the decision on the purpose and the essential elements were established by the holding company (data of data subjects determined for a marketing campaign with the purpose of leveraging sales of services, for a certain period). In this case, the Brazilian subsidiary YANKEE is the data processor. This is because it processes data exclusively in accordance with XRAY's instructions, which were defined in a contractual instrument signed between the parties.
> With regard to the processing of its employees' data, when processing payroll, for instance, the Brazilian subsidiary YANKEE will be considered the data controller.
> On the other hand, if the holding company XRAY and the Brazilian subsidiary YANKEE develop a new service for the Brazilian public, jointly defining the purposes and essential elements of the processing, they will act as joint controllers in relation to this operation."

333. To best illustrate a practical situation of joint controllership, it is worth mentioning Case C-40/17 from the Court of Justice of the European Union (CJEU). This case involved *Fashion ID* company, which has embedded on its website a social plugin that allowed the personal data of a visitor to the website to be transferred to the provider of the plugin, which was Facebook.

334. In such case, the Court has decided the following:

> The operator of a website, such as Fashion ID GmbH & Co. KG, that embeds on that website a social plugin causing the browser of a visitor to that website

to request content from the provider of that plugin and, to that end, to transmit to that provider personal data of the visitor can be considered to be a controller, within the meaning of Article 2(d) of Directive 95/46. That liability is, however, limited to the operation or set of operations involving the processing of personal data in respect of which it actually determines the purposes and means, that is to say, the collection and disclosure by transmission of the data at issue.[84]

335. As observed in the decision, since both parties were beneficiated by the same processing activity and had jointly determined the means and the extent of the processing, they should be considered joint controllers.

84. Document 62017CJ0040. Available on https://eur-lex.europa.eu/legal-content/EN/TXT/?uri=CELEX%3A62017CJ0040. Access on Nov. 7, 2022.

Chapter 3. National Rules Regarding Processors

336. The ANPD highlights the decision-making power as the main difference between the controller and the processor, the operator being responsible for acting within limits set by the controller's decisions, that is, in accordance with the purposes established by the latter.

337. The ANPD guideline provides the following information:

4. PROCESSOR

4.1 Legal Definition

51. The processor is the agent responsible for carrying out the data processing on behalf of the controller and according to the purpose delimited by the controller. The legal definition is found in Article 5, clause VII of the LGPD:

Natural or legal person, whether of public or private law, which performs the processing of personal data on behalf of the controller

52. In this same sense is the provision of Article 39 of LGPD:

The processor must carry out the processing according to the instructions provided by the controller, who will verify compliance with its own instructions and the regulations on the matter.

53. The above provision implies saying that the processor may only process the data for the purpose previously established by the controller. This demonstrates the main difference between the controller and the processor, namely, the power of decision: the processor can only act within the limits of the purposes determined by the controller.
54. It is also worth highlighting some of the obligations of the processor: (i) to follow the controller's instructions; (ii) to sign contracts that establish, among other matters, the regime of activities and responsibilities with the controller; (iii) to make the controller aware in the event of a contract with a sub-processor.
55. The concept and scope of the processor's activities also indicate the importance of contractual definitions for the relationship between controller and processor. Even though the LGPD does not expressly determine that the controller and the processor must enter into a contract on data processing, such adjustment is shown to be a good data processing practice, since contractual clauses impose limits on the processor's actions, set objective parameters for the allocation of responsibilities between the parties, and reduce the risks and uncertainties arising from the operation.
56. The items that may be contractually defined are the object, duration, nature and purpose of the data processing, the types of personal data involved and the rights and obligations and responsibilities related to compliance with the LGPD.

57. Finally, within the processor's scope of action, it is important to say that it may define non-essential elements of the processing, such as technical measures.

4.2 Types of processors

58. According to the LGPD, individuals and legal persons of public and private law may act as processors. Most of the time, the processor is a legal person, which is contracted by the controller to carry out the data processing as instructed by the latter. However, there is no obstacle for a natural person contracted as a service provider for a specific purpose to be considered a data processor.
59. In the case of a legal person, it should be noted that the organization or company is understood as the processing agent, so that its employees merely represent it. As explained in topic 2.2 and analogously to the definition of controller, the legal definition of processor should also not be understood as a standard of internal distribution of competences and responsibilities.
60. In this scenario, employees, managers, partners, public servants and other natural persons that integrate the legal person and whose acts express the performance of the latter must not be considered processors, considering that the processor will always be a person distinct from the controller, that is, who does not act as a professional subordinated to the latter or as a member of its bodies.

4.3 Liability

61. Although the controller has the primary responsibility and the processor must act on its behalf, Article 37[85] of the LGPD determines that both share obligations and, consequently, the responsibility to keep the register of processing operations. In addition, pursuant to Article 42[86] of the LGPD, both have the obligation of redress if they cause property, moral, individual or collective damage to others within their respective spheres of action.
62. However, it should be noted that, as a rule, the obligations and responsibilities of the controller and the processor are distinct, as they are determined according to the role exercised by each in the processing of personal data. Thus, the joint and several liability established by Subsection I, Paragraph 1 of Article 42 of the LGPD,[87] provided for the cases of damages caused due to irregular processing performed by a processor (for failing to comply with the obligations of the legislation or failing to comply controller's instructions), may be considered as an exceptionality, since as a rule the responsibility lies with the controller. In principle, this is the only case in which the processor is equated to the controller.

85. Article 37. The controller and the processor shall keep records of personal data processing operations carried out by them, especially when based on legitimate interest.
86. *See* n. 5 on item n° 14.
87. *See ibid.*

4.4 Examples

Example 8—E-commerce

In an online book-selling channel, which has several payment methods, the channel that makes the sale is the controller of the personal data, while each payment service available will be a different processor, such as, for example, the credit card company, a fintech, the bank in case of bank transfer, among others. The processor of that transaction, whatever it may be, may not use the data provided for new purposes other than those determined by the controller.

Example 9—Call center

Company XRAY is responsible for its customers' data and passes it on to an outsourced call center company, Zulu, which receives the information. Xray is the holding company, and the outsourced call center Zulu is the processor, which will process customer data on behalf of XRAY. If it performs data processing outside of what was directed by the controller, the ZULU company may be held liable.

Example 10—Public servants

An autarchy, an indirect public administration entity with its own legal personality, wishes to use a new software to improve the management of the institution's employees. For this purpose, the entity's Corporate Management Secretariat delegates to the Personnel Management Board (DGP) the task of determining the means by which this software will be implemented. After a few meetings, the DGP decides to hire the outsourced company SIERRA to develop the software in partnership with the internal team of the Information Technology Directorate (DTI).

338. Although the delegation of the decision regarding the means to the Personnel Management Board (DGP) may suggest that this directorate acts as a data processor, this is not the correct analysis: as DGP is an administrative unit of the municipality, the internal delegation does not change the role of the processing agent, since, as exposed, the processor will always be a person distinct from the controller. The same reasoning applies to Information Technology Directorate (DTI). Thus, the municipality will be the controller, and SIERRA will be the processor. The Secretariat and the Directorates, as well as their respective employees, are merely organizational units of the data controller, for which reason they are not characterized as processing agents.

5. SUB-PROCESSOR

5.1 Legal Definition

63. Formally, the LGPD, with regard to processing agents, has defined only the figures of the controller and processor (Article 5, items VI, VII and IX), according to the following excerpt:

Art. 5 For the purposes of this Law, it is considered:

VI—controller: natural or legal person, whether of public or private law, responsible for decisions regarding the processing of personal data;

VII—processor: natural or legal person, whether of public or private law, which performs the processing of personal data on behalf of the controller
(...)
IX—processing agents: the controller and the processor; (our emphasis)

64. Although there is no concept of sub-processor in the LGPD, the theme may be used as an analysis parameter for understanding more complex chains of data processing.
65. This is because the lack of the concept of sub-processor in the LGPD does not make it impossible or illegal for it to exist or to have functions, competencies and responsibility in the Brazilian personal data protection environment, mainly because it may perform the function of processor in subordination to another processor. Having said this, it is important to know that the sub-processor is the one hired by the processor to assist him in performing the processing of personal data on behalf of the controller. The sub-processor's direct relationship is with the processor and not with the controller. However, regardless of the institutional arrangements between processor and sub-processor, for the purposes of the LGPD, both may perform, depending on the specific case, the function of processor and be accountable before the ANPD.
66. Considering that the processor performs the processing of personal data on behalf of the controller, it is to be assumed that the relationship between them is founded on trust.
67. In this sense, it is recommended that the processor, when contracting the sub-processor, obtains formal authorization (generic or specific) from the controller, which may even be included in the contract signed between the parties. This measure aims to avoid the perception that, when contracting the sub-processor, the processor has executed the data processing in breach of the controller's instructions, which could attract responsibilities to the processor which are normally exclusive to the controller.

Art. 42—The controller or processor which, in performing activities involving the processing of personal data, causes pecuniary, moral, individual or collective damage to another person, in violation of the personal data protection legislation, is obliged to compensate it.
§ In order to ensure effective compensation to the data subject:
I—the processor shall be jointly and severally liable for the damage caused by the processing when it fails to comply with the obligations of the personal data protection legislation or when it has not followed the lawful instructions of the controller, in which case the processor shall be equivalent to the controller, except in the cases of exemptions provided in art. 43 of this Law;
Article 28.—Processor.
(...)
2. The processor shall not engage another processor without prior specific or general written authorization of the controller. In the case of general written authorization, the processor shall inform the controller of any intended changes concerning the addition or replacement of other processors, thereby giving the controller the opportunity to object to such changes.
(...)

4. Where a processor engages another processor for carrying out specific processing activities on behalf of the controller, the same data protection obligations as set out in the contract or other legal act between the controller and the processor as referred to in paragraph 3 shall be imposed on that other processor by contract or other legal act under Union or Member State law, in particular providing sufficient guarantees to implement appropriate technical and organisational measures in such a manner that the processing will meet the requirements of this Regulation. Where that other processor fails to fulfil its data protection obligations, the initial processor shall remain fully responsible to the controller for the performance of that other processor's obligations.

69. With regard to responsibilities, the sub-processor may be equal to the processor before the LGPD in relation to the activities it has been contracted to perform. Thus, there is an expansion of the chain of joint and several liability provided in art. 42, §1, I[88] of LGPD.

5.2 Examples

Example 11—Outsourcing Cloud Storage Service
ALPHA wants to hire a market researcher to leverage its sales. To do so, it hires the research company BRAVO, which sends the results to ALPHA.
With the authorization of ALPHA, BRAVO hires the cloud storage services CHARLIE.
Company ALPHA may be considered a controller since it is verified that the following requirements were met: (i) company A had decision-making power regarding data processing; (ii) the essential elements of the processing were defined by company A: purpose, data subjects (e.g., women in the age range of 20 to 30 years, residents in Brasília/DF), types of data (e.g., name, age, address, food preference), etc.
Although it may decide on the techniques to be employed in the data processing to generate the research results, the research company BRAVO carries out the data processing in accordance with the purpose and instructions determined by the company ALPHA, acting, therefore, as processor.
The CHARLIE company acts according to the guidelines of the BRAVO company and would therefore be a sub-processor. We recommend that BRAVO obtain formal authorization from ALPHA for subcontracting CHARLIE.
Example 12—Web tool and storage service
GOLF and its subsidiaries (hereinafter referred to as "GOLF Group") start collecting registration and consumption data from their customers. However, the storage and collection of this data is carried out using ECHO's web tool.
The GOLF Group informed which data it wants to collect, for how long it intends to keep them and what kind of processing it intends to do with these data, therefore, it is the controller.

88. *See ibid.*

ECHO, in turn, makes some technical decisions about access protocols, storage, backup, protection against intrusions, all according to the security specifications required by the GOLF group. ECHO is the processor.
This same ECHO company, realizing that the volume of data to be stored is superior to the capacity of its internal databases, with the authorization of the Group, contracts a storage service with the company FOXTROT. The FOXTROT company is a sub-processor.
Example 13—Store Draw
The KILO shop organizes a prize draw and, to take part, customers fill in a registration form with some personal information. The data and the purpose of processing are defined by the KILO shop, which is the controller.
The storage and collection of these data are carried out, by employees of the shop KILO, in the system of the company LIMA. The company LIMA is the processor.
At the end of the registration period, KILO hires OSCAR to carry out the draw using the data stored by LIMA. OSCAR is also a processor, due to its direct relationship to the parent company, KILO.

339. Beyond what was presented, especially concerning the contract between controller and processor, it is also important to mention some of the best practices which shall be contractually adopted to confirm the parties' relation:

– the possibility of adding sub-processors to the processing and the standards that they must comply with in order to perform the activities following the controller's orders;
– the means by which the processor shall notify the controller about security incidents that could interfere with the processing activities;
– the forms with which the processor shall receive any contact from data subjects and how to answer and transmit it to the controller;
– the level of security and the standards that should be followed during the execution of the processing activity;
– the orientations relative to international transfer of data;
– the possibility for the controller to conduct audits in the processor whenever it deems necessary for the sake of the processing activity.

340. As seen, to keep its position as a processor and not be confused with a joint controller or even with another independent controller, the processor shall strictly follow what was determined by the controller for the activity and respect the contract provisions.

Chapter 4. Security Obligations

341. Security is one of the principles that must be observed in the processing of personal data, pursuant to Article 6, VII, of the LGPD:

> Art. 6 ° The activities of processing personal data must observe the good faith and the following principles:
> (...)
> VII—security: use of technical and administrative measures able to protect personal data from unauthorized access and accidental or unlawful situations of destruction, loss, alteration, communication or dissemination;

342. As shown in the following articles, it is up to the processing agents to adopt the necessary security measures to ensure the protection of the data subjects, and the ANPD may have the minimum technical standards recommended to be adopted:

> Art. 46. Agents of processing shall adopt security, technical and administrative measures able to protect personal data from unauthorized access and accidental or unlawful situations of destruction, loss, alteration, communication or any form of improper or unlawful processing.
> § 1—The national authority may have on minimum technical standards to make applicable the provisions of the caput of this article, considering the nature of the information processed, the specific characteristics of the processing and the current state of the technology, especially in the case of sensitive personal data, as well as the principles provided for in the caput of art. 6 of this Law.
> § 2—The measures dealing with the caput of this article shall be observed from the stage of conception of the product or service until its implementation.
> Art. 47. Agents of processing or any other person who intervenes in one of the stages of the processing is obliged to ensure the security of the information provided for in this Law in relation to personal data, even after its termination.
> Art. 48. The controller shall notify the national authority and the holder of the occurrence of a security incident which may result in significant risk or damage to the holders.

343. Especially regarding the above-mentioned Article 46, it is essential to establish that the security obligations are not completely linked to the results of the absence of any kind of security incident. This is because, as it is already common knowledge, there is no way to totally guarantee the security of an application. Then, what is demanded of processor agents is that they take preventive security measures aligned to what is presented on LGPD and that they report the whole situation to the national authority and subjects in a timely fashion.

344. In compliance with its guiding role, the ANPD has issued an Information Security Guide for Small Treatment Agents, considering that these agents, due to their size and possible limitations, often do not have among their staff people specialized in information security and need to improve it in relation to the processing of personal data. The guide indicates administrative measures and information security techniques and a checklist to facilitate the visualization of the suggestions that will be adopted. Free translations of the recommendations contained in the checklist will be inserted below.

CHECKLIST OF SECURITY MEASURES FOR SMALL PROCESSING AGENTS:

INFORMATION SECURITY POLICY

- Establish a simplified information security policy that establishes controls related to the processing of personal data, such as backups, use of passwords, access to information, data sharing, software update, use of e-mail and use of antivirus.
- Conduct periodic reviews of information security policy.
- Manage contracts and acquisitions with compliance with the proper processing of personal data.

AWARENESS AND TRAINING

- To make employee awareness, through training and campaigns about their obligations and responsibilities related to the processing of personal data as provided by the LGPD and ANPD regulation.
- Inform and sensitize all employees of the organization, especially those directly involved in the data processing activity, about the legal obligations existing in the LGPD and in standards and guidelines issued by the ANPD.
- Inform employees about:

  how to use security controls for IT systems related to daily work;
  how to avoid becoming victims of everyday security incidents, such as virus contamination or phishing attacks, which may occur, for example, by clicking on incoming links in the form of pop-up promotional offers or on unknown links that arrive by e-mail;
  keep physical documents containing personal data inside drawers, not on desks;
  not share workstation logins and access passwords;
  lock computers when move away from workstations to prevent undue access from third parties;
  guidelines of information security policy.

- Create an organizational environment that encourages users of company systems, both customers and employees, to report incidents and vulnerabilities detected.

CONTRACT MANAGEMENT

– Establish contracts with information security clauses that ensure the protection of personal data, such as:

rules for suppliers and partners;
rules on shares;
controller-processor relationships;
guidelines on the processing to be carried out not allowing treatments incompatible with the controller's guidelines.

– Sign non-disclosure agreement (NDA) with company employees.

ACCESS CONTROL

– Implement an access control system applicable to all users, with permission levels in proportion to the need to work with the system and to access personal data.
– Configure features in the access control system that can detect and not allow the use of passwords that do not respect a certain level of complexity.
– Implement an adequate password management, establishing controls such as:

avoid the use of standard passwords provided by purchased software or hardware vendors;
use only complex passwords to access applications and other computer systems;
not reuse passwords.

– Prohibit the sharing of accounts or passwords between employees.
– Apply the principle of least privilege (need to know).
– Use multi-factor authentication to access systems or databases that contain personal data.
– Implement an access control system applicable to all users who access the IT system (if the processing agent has an internal network of computers).
– Collect and process only personal data that is actually necessary to achieve the purposes of the processing for the intended purpose, minimizing data collection.
– Implement pseudonymization solutions, such as encryption, to encrypt personal data.
– Guide employees not to disable or ignore workstation security settings.
– Avoid transferring personal data from workstations to external storage devices such as USB sticks and external hard drives.
– Inventory and encrypt data from external devices and store it in safe locations.
– Perform offline, periodic backups and store them securely.
– Format and overwrite physical media that contains personal data before discarding it, or, when it is not possible to overwrite, destroy physical media.

- Establish in the service contract the record of destruction/disposal (if the processing agent uses third party services for disposal).
- Use encrypted connections (TLS/HTTPS) or end-to-end encryption applications for communication services.
- Install and maintain a firewall system and/or use a Web Application Firewall (WAF—Application Filter).
- Protect emails via adoption of AntiSpam tools, e-mail filters and, integrate the antivirus into the email system.
- Remove any sensitive data and other personal data that is unnecessarily made available on public networks.

VULNERABILITY MANAGEMENT

- Periodically update all systems and applications used, keeping them in their updated version (install security patches made available by vendors).
- Periodically adopt and update antivirus software and antimalware.
- Perform periodic antivirus scans on the devices and systems used.

MOBILE DEVICES

- Use multi-factor authentication techniques to control access to mobile devices—such as smartphones and laptops.
- Separate mobile devices for private use from those of institutional use, when possible.

CLOUD SERVICES

- Sign a service-level agreement with the cloud service provider, covering the security of the stored data.
- Assess whether the service offered by the cloud service provider meets the other established information security requirements.
- Review the requirements for user access to each cloud service used.
- Use multi-factor authentication techniques to access cloud services related to personal data.

Chapter 5. Data Protection Office or Similar Functions

345. The Brazilian DPO ("encarregado de proteção de dados") will be appointed by the controller to act as the main point of contact between the data subjects and the ANPD. Its duties are established in the LGPD; however, the ANPD may establish complementary standards on its definition and attributions, including the hypothesis of its dismissal.

346. On this topic, the ANPD guideline provides:

> 6. Data Protection Officer
>
> 6.1 Legal Definition
>
> 70. As per Article 41 of the LGPD, the data controller must appoint an officer for the processing of personal data. In the course of his or her duties, the DPO can play an important role in fostering and disseminating the culture of personal data protection in the organization, for example, by receiving requests from data subjects and the national authority and taking action, or advising employees and contractors on practices to be taken in relation to the protection of personal data
>
> Art. 41 The controller shall appoint a data protection officer.
>
> 71. Unlike other foreign data protection legislation, the LGPD has not determined under what circumstances an organization must appoint a data protection officer. Thus, it should be assumed, as a general rule, that every organization should appoint a person to take on this role.
> 72. However, according to paragraph 3 of Article 41,[89] the ANPD published Resolution CD/ANPD No. 2, January 27, 2022, which approves the Regulation of Application of the LGPD for Small Treatment Agents, which brings hypothesis of exemption from the need to indicate the DPO.
> 73. Article 41 of the LGPD makes no distinction between public and private institutions, so it is important that both are aware of their obligation to appoint a data protection officer. In this regard, Article 23, III,[90] reinforces the need for a data controller to be appointed by public bodies and entities.
> 74. The LGPD also does not distinguish whether the data protection officer must be a natural or legal person, and whether it must be an employee of

89. Article 41. The controller shall appoint a data protection officer to be in charge of processing personal data.
§3 The national authority may establish complementary rules about the definition and the duties of the data protection officer, including situations in which the appointment of such person may be waived, according to the nature and the size of the entity or the volume of data processing operations.
90. *See* n. 11 on item n° 23.

the organization or an external agent. Considering international good practices, the data protection officer may be either an employee of the institution or an external agent, of natural or legal nature. It is recommended that the data protection officer be appointed by a formal act, such as a service contract or an administrative act.

75. As good practice, it is considered important that the data protection officer be free in the performance of his duties. As regards their professional qualifications, these should be defined by means of a value judgment made by the appointing controller, considering knowledge of data protection and information security at a level that meets the needs of the organization's personal data processing operations.
76. It is also important to note that the LGPD does not prohibit the data protection officer from being supported by a data protection team. Rather, considering good practice, it is important that the data protection officer has adequate resources to carry out its activities, which may include human resources. Other resources that should be considered are time (appropriate deadlines), finances and infrastructure.
77. While the LGPD does not prevent the same data protection officer from acting on behalf of different organisations, it is important that the data protection officer be able to perform his duties effectively. Thus, before appointing a data protection officer, the controller should consider whether he will be able to meet the controller's and other organisations' demands at the same time. The responsibility for personal data processing activities remains with the controller or the data processor, as set out in Article 42 of the LGPD.

6.2 Duties of the data protection officer.

78. According to § 2 of art. 41,[91] the data protection officer has the following attributions:
    - accept complaints and communications from data subjects, provide clarifications and adopt measures;
    - receive communications from the national authority and adopt measures;
    - to guide the entity's employees and contractors as to the practices to be adopted in relation to the protection of personal data; and
    - perform the other attributions determined by the controller or established in complementary norms.

---

91. Article 41. The controller shall appoint a data protection officer.
    §2 Data Protection Officer's activities consist of:

    I — accepting complaints and communications from data subjects, providing explanations and adopting measures;
    II — receiving communications from the national authority and adopting measures;
    III — orienting entity's employees and contractors regarding practices to be taken in relation to personal data protection; and
    IV — carrying out other duties as determined by the controller or set forth in complementary rules.

79. Because it acts as a point of contact with data subjects and the ANPD, it is important that the contact details of the data protection officer are easily accessible, pursuant to § 1 of Article 41[92] of the LGPD:

The identity and contact details of the data protection officer must be publicly disclosed in a clear and objective manner, preferably on the controller's website.

80. In alignment with § 3 of art. 41,[93] the ANPD may establish complementary rules on the definition and attributions of the data protection officer.
81. It should be emphasized that there is no need, in view of the absence of legal or regulatory provision, for communication or registration of the identity and contact details of the data protection officer before ANPD.

347. Published in January by the ANPD, the Resolution CD/ANPD No. 2 of January 27, 2022, brought the possibility of no indication of a Data Protection Officer in the case of data processing by small-size processing agents, mostly being small-size businesses that deal with data processing. But not every small business could be considered a small-size processing agent; conditions imposed by the law need to be fulfilled to be considered this kind of processing agent. The conditions being:

I — Micro and small businesses, according to art. 41 of Law No. 14,195, of August 26, 2021, and the entrepreneur referred to in art. 966 of Law No. 10.406, of January 10, 2002 (Civil Code), including the individual micro-entrepreneur duly registered in the Commercial Companies Registry or in the Civil Registry of Legal Entities, which fall under the terms of art. 3 and 18-A, §1 of Complementary Law No. 123, of December 14, 2006;
II — Startups that meet the criteria set forth in Chapter II of Complementary Law No. 182 of June 1, 2021;
III — Publicly accessible areas.

348. And all these entities, to be considered small-size processing agents, could not:

I — perform high-risk treatment for the data subjects, except in the case provided for in art. 8;
II — earn gross revenue higher than the limit established in Article 3, II, of Complementary Law No. 123, of 2006 or, in the case of startups, in Article 4, § 1, I, of Complementary Law No. 182, of 2021; or
III — belong to a de facto or de jure economic group whose global revenue exceeds the limits referred to in item II, as the case may be.

349. Only processing agents that would fill all these conditions could be considered small-size processing agents and would not be required to point out a DPO,

92. *See* n. 21 on item 60.
93. *See* n. 23 on item 69.

and if they did so, it could be considered a good practice of data protection and privacy governance, which might as well bring out all responsibilities for regular-size processing agents.

350. Finally, the ANPD points out that materials produced and published are subject to comments and contributions by civil society on a continuous basis and will be constantly updated as new regulations and understandings are established and published.

Part VI. Codes of Conduct and Certification

351. This part of the book aims to explain the codes of conduct and certifications in the Brazilian data protection law (LGPD). The following chapter contains the analysis of these instruments in the GDPR and LGPD to provide a better understanding of their use to demonstrate compliance with privacy laws and adequate levels of security to protect personal data and allow international transfer by controllers and processors. However, the topic dealt with in this chapter is still awaiting ANPD regulation.

352. With the entry into force of the Brazilian data protection law (LGPD) in September 2020, a new regulatory framework was established in Brazil, aimed at protecting the fundamental rights of freedom, privacy, and the free development of the personality, establishing rights of data subjects and duties for controllers and processors of personal data.

353. Its application (Article 3. LGPD) will be given to any processing operation carried out by a natural person or by a legal entity governed by public or private law, regardless of the means, the country of its headquarters, or the country where the data are located, provided that:

I — the treatment operation is carried out in the national territory;
II — the processing activity has as its objective the offer or supply of goods or services or the processing of data of individuals located in the national territory; or
III — the personal data object of the processing has been collected in the national territory.

354. Its application and extraterritorial scope hypotheses are like the GDPR application hypotheses, not applying only to processing operations carried out in Brazil, but whenever personal data is collected in the national territory, or there is an offer of products and services for individuals located in the country.

355. Among the obligations imposed by the LGPD on processing agents are those to frame the processing of personal data and sensitive personal data in one of the legal bases, observe the principles for the processing of personal data, safeguard and enable the exercise of rights of data subjects, mitigate risks to the individual rights and freedoms of individuals caused by the processing, implement security measures, a privacy governance program and the compliance with the privacy by design framework.

356. In this regard, the principle of responsibility and accountability, provided for in Article 6, X of the LGPD, imposes on the processing agents that, in addition to adopting effective measures capable of proving compliance with and compliance with personal data protection rules, they must be able to demonstrate them, including about their effectiveness.

357. In this sense, Article 50 of the LGPD enables controllers and processors, within the scope of their competences, individually or through associations, formulated rules of standards by the activity of processing personal data.

358. These "Codes of Conduct" must establish the conditions of organization, operating regime, and procedures, including complaints and petitions from data subjects, safety rules, technical standards, specific obligations for those involved in the processing, educational actions, the internal mechanisms for supervision, and risk mitigation and other aspects related to the processing of personal data.

359. Therefore, there is an opening for sectorial self-regulation by processing agents with codes of good practices and governance that should be able to demonstrate the effectiveness of their privacy governance program at the request of ANPD or another entity responsible for promoting compliance with good practices or codes of conduct independently (Article 50, §2, II of the LGPD).

360. As discussed above, the extraterritorial reach of the LGPD will require even greater care by the processing agents if personal data are somehow transferred, as in the case of contracting suppliers and service providers abroad, such as services of cloud hosting or multinationals.

361. In these cases also, to ensure an adequate level of data protection during processing and to protect the data subject from unauthorized access or accidental or unlawful situations of destruction, loss, alteration, communication, or any form of inappropriate or unlawful processing, as well as compliance with the legal bases, data processing principles and rights of data subjects, the LGPD provides in Chapter V on the International Transfer of Personal Data.

362. Article 33 of the LGPD provides for the situations in which the international transfer is authorized, and among them, we observe in item II, letter "d," that when the controller offers and proves guarantees of compliance with the principles, the data subjects rights of data subjects and the data protection regime provided for in the LGPD, in the form of regularly issued seals, certificates and codes of conduct, making the international transfer of data lawful.

§1. Codes of Conduct and Certifications at GDPR

363. In comparison, in the GDPR, codes of conduct and certifications are provided for in Section 5, precisely in Articles 40 to 43. However, the topic is also addressed in several considerations; for example, to reinforce transparency and compliance with the GDPR, the regulation seeks to encourage the creation of certification procedures and data protection seals and marks, allowing data subjects to quickly assess the level of data protection of relevant products and services.

364. In addition, guidance on taking appropriate action and on proving compliance by controllers and processors can be obtained using approved codes of conduct, approved certifications, guidance provided by the Board or directions provided by a DPO about identifying best practices for risk mitigation (Recital 77).

365. Another important function of the codes of conduct and certifications provided for in the GDPR (Recital 81) is related to the demonstration of compliance of processors that demonstrate to the controller that it has sufficient guarantees regarding the implementation of technical and organizational measures of information security that comply with the GDPR requirements during the hiring process.

366. Likewise, controllers can also use codes of conduct and certifications as an element to demonstrate compliance with the requirements of the regulation (Article 24 (3)).

367. Concerning these instruments of demonstration of compliance, in summary, Article 40 concerns the elaboration of codes of conduct intended to contribute to the correct application of the GDPR, bearing in mind the characteristics of the different processing sectors and the specific needs of micro-, small- and medium-sized companies, while Article 41, provides for the supervision of compliance with codes of conduct by a body that has an adequate level of competence about the object of the code and is accredited for this by the competent Data Protection Authority (DPA).

368. Besides, Article 42 provides for the creation of certification procedures in the field of data protection, as well as data protection seals and marks, to prove the compliance of the processing operations of controllers and processors with the GDPR.

369. Finally, Article 43 provides that a certification body that has an adequate level of competence in data protection matters may issue and renew the certification after informing DPA so that it can exercise its competences whenever necessary. The Member States of the European Union ensure that these certification bodies are accredited:

(a) By the competent supervisory authority [...];

(b) By the national accreditation body, designated under Regulation (EC) No. 765/2008 of the European Parliament and the Council, in accordance with EN-ISO/IEC 17065/2012 and with the additional requirements established by the authority of control [...].

370. Codes of conduct are tools voluntarily adopted by processing agents, allowing certain sectors to identify and solve the main data protection challenges with the DPA guarantee that the code and its monitoring are appropriate, as defined by Information Commission Officer (ICO)[94] on its website.

371. By signing a code of conduct, controllers and processors can ensure effective application of the GDPR and, in doing so, establish operational compliance standards that should help reduce levels of noncompliance by being more transparent and accountable with processing personal data by considering the specific requirements of data processing carried out in a specific sector, transmitting to the data subject a message of confidence regarding the personal data.

372. On the other hand, as a way of attesting the ability to comply with the GDPR and attest its compliance, the certification can help to demonstrate data protection practices to companies, data subjects, and DPAs, as it makes it possible to demonstrate that data processing complies with the requirements of the GDPR, following the principle of responsibility.

373. Codes of conduct and certifications are valid instruments capable of validating and attesting to the compliance of controls and processors, given that signing a code of conduct or obtaining certification by a processing agent can help you demonstrate the implementation privacy by design in its processing operations, which has physical, technical and organizational security measures capable of guaranteeing the security of personal data and supporting the transfer of personal data to third countries or international organizations (Article 46, No. 2, letter f)).

§2. Codes of Conduct and Certifications in the LGPD

374. As with the GDPR, in Brazil, codes of conduct are tools that can be voluntarily adopted by processing agents, allowing certain sectors to identify and resolve the main data protection challenges and, subsequently, have these practices ratified by the ANPD while the certifications are a certificate of capacity, compliance or both, to carry out the processing of personal data following frameworks and current legislation.

94. Information Commission Officer. Codes of Conduct. What Are Codes of Conduct?. Available at: https://ico.org.uk/for-organisations/guide-to-data-protection/guide-to-the-general-data-protection-regulation-gdpr/accountability-and-governance/codes-of-conduct/. Access on Nov. 27, 2021.

375. Contrary to what can be seen in the GDPR, the LGPD was succinct in providing in Article 35 that the possibilities provided for in item II, Article 33, relating to international transfers, will be regulated by the ANPD; let us see:

> Art. 35. The definition of the content of standard contractual clauses, as well as the verification of specific contractual clauses for a given transfer, global corporate standards or seals, certificates, and codes of conduct, referred to in item II of the caput of art. 33 of this Law, will be carried out by the national authority.
> § 1 To verify the provisions of the caput of this article, the requirements, conditions, and minimum guarantees for the transfer must be considered, in compliance with the rights, guarantees, and principles of this Law.
> § 2 In the analysis of contractual clauses, documents, or global corporate standards submitted for approval by the national authority, additional information may be required or steps to verify the processing operations may be required, when necessary.
> § 3 The national authority may designate certification bodies to carry out the provisions of the caput of this article, which will remain under its supervision under the terms defined in the regulation.
> § 4 The acts performed by a certification body may be reviewed by the national authority and, if not in compliance with this Law, submitted for review or canceled.
> § 5 Sufficient guarantees of compliance with the general principles of protection and rights of data subject referred to in the caput of this article will also be analyzed in accordance with the technical and organizational measures adopted by the processor, in accordance with the provisions of §§ 1 and 2 of art. 46 of this Law.

376. The ANPD Ordinance nº. 35, which makes public the Regulatory Agenda of the ANPD for the biennium 2023/2024,[95] was published in the Official Gazette of the Union on November 8, 2022. The Regulatory Agenda for the next biennium has established twenty actions, and the topic of international transfer of personal data was cited as action number four within phase 1.

377. The regulatory agenda consists of a planning tool of the autarchy to guarantee more transparency, predictability and efficiency to its regulatory process, and its elaboration took into consideration the contributions obtained from the public's manifestations by means of subsidy taking carried out for certain matters, to define the most important themes to be discussed next year.

95. National Data Protection Authority. Ordinance No. 35, of Nov. 8, 2022, makes the regulatory agenda for the 2023–2024 biennium public. Available at: https://www.gov.br/anpd/pt-br/assuntos/noticias/anpd-publica-agenda-regulatoria-2023-2024. Access on Jan. 24, 2023.

§3. PERSPECTIVES FOR REGULATION

378. In the LGPD, it is possible to see that the Brazilian legislator was directly inspired by the guidelines provided in the GDPR for international transfers, with little innovations in the authorizing hypotheses, clearly in search of an eventual adequacy decision; however, it briefly described that authorizing hypotheses of the international transfer will be regulated in the future by ANPD.

379. It is true that, in the forthcoming regulation, certain requirements, conditions, and minimum guarantees for the transfer will be considered and analyzed by ANPD based on the rights, guarantees, and principles provided for in the LGPD.

380. The national authority may designate certification bodies to carry out the provisions of the caput of this article, which will remain under its supervision under the terms defined in the regulation. Acts performed by a certification body may be reviewed by the national authority and, if not in compliance with this Law, subject to review or cancellation.

381. In this sense, on September 12, 2020, the Brazilian Association of Technical Standards (ABNT) presented its new certification program based on the ISO/IEC 27001: 2014 and ISO/IEC 27701:2020 standards so that companies can prove their compliance with the LGPD, which have controls that if implemented, would comply with part of the Brazilian Law.

382. It is important to remember that the standards provided for in the ISO/IEC 27001 specifies the requirements for establishing, implementing, maintaining, and continuing to improve an information security management system and include requirements for the assessment and processing of information security risks tailored to the needs of an organization.

383. The Privacy Information Management System (PIMS) was established by the ISO/IEC 27701:2020 standard, which is an Extension to ISO/IEC 27001 and ISO/IEC 27002 ABNT NBR ISO/IEC 27002 for privacy information management. The standard brought additional guidelines and requirements for controllers and processors, complementing the Information Security Management System.

384. In Brazil, this certification was called the Privacy Management Systems and Personal Data Protection Certification by ABNT.

385. Organizations wishing to obtain certification for the Certification of Management Systems for the Protection and Privacy of Personal Data must first carry out a self-assessment that must be forwarded to ABNT to start the certification process. Self-assessment is carried out through a checklist prepared by the working group that created the certification program.

386. After this step, a face-to-face compliance audit is scheduled to verify that the items provided in the checklists are implemented and working correctly. Once approved by the auditors, the certification is issued and will be valid for three years; maintenance audits must be carried out every twelve months.

387. However, the certification of the Personal Data Protection and Privacy Management Systems Certification does not have LGPD approval, which does not mean that it will be approved in the future, being adopted voluntarily by organizations that wish to certify their processes based on the standard established by ISO/IEC 27701.

388. The protection of personal data is still a new issue in Brazil, and due to the gaps left by the legislator in the LGPD, several issues still need to be regulated by ANPD, such as the case of international transfers. Thus, it is not possible to say that organizations are fully in compliance with the law but that, based on good faith, they adopt all available and possible measures that are within their power to implement technical and organizational control measures to protect illicit data processing and strengthen governance in privacy.

Part VII. International Transfers

Chapter 1. General Principles

389. This chapter aims to explain the general principles for the transfer of personal data under the Brazilian General Data Protection Law. Its content approaches the different mechanisms made available by the law to make international transfers possible. A detailed analysis of each transfer mechanism is made, reflecting the actual Brazilian scenario of legal uncertainty and the obstacles faced by the processing agents.

§1. Data Protection and Privacy: Brazilian General Data Protection Legislation

390. The LGPD, which was fully based on the GDPR, created a regulation for the use, protection, and transfer of personal data in Brazil in the public and private spheres and established in a clear way who are the parts involved and which are their attributions, responsibilities, and penalties.

391. The LGPD regulates in a strict way about international data transfers and restricts the transfer of personal data to countries or international organizations outside the Brazilian territory to protect its citizens' rights. These restrictions are applied to all transfers, no matter their size or the way they are carried out.

392. Laid down in Chapter V, Articles 33 to 36, are the conditions required to allow transfers of personal data to third countries or international organizations, guaranteeing the same level of protection that the legislation offers to its inhabitants.

393. The conditions laid down for international transfers must be complied with by the controller and the processor, including for onward transfers from third countries or international organizations to other third countries or international organizations.

394. The "toolkit" made available by the Legislation for international data transfers comprises: Adequacy Decisions; Specific Contractual Clauses for a Given Transfer; Standard Contractual Clauses (SCCs), Binding Corporate Rules (BCRs); Seals, Certificates and Codes of Conduct; Bilateral Agreements and Derogations.

395. Adequacy Decisions consist of decisions adopted by the Brazilian ANPD allowing the flow of personal data with third countries or international organizations without further safeguards. This is a basic and raw notion, noting that more details and explanations on this topic will be later approached.

396. In the absence of an adequacy decision adopted by the ANPD, the LGPD offers the alternative of appropriate safeguards provided by the controller in its Article 33, II.

397. II—where the controller provides and demonstrates guarantees of compliance with the principles, rights of the data subject and data protection regime established in this Law, in the form of:

a) specific contractual sections for a given transfer;
b) standard contractual sections;
c) global corporate rules;
d) seals, certificates and codes of conduct regularly issued.

398. If there are no adequacy decisions or appropriate safeguards, there is still the mechanism of bilateral agreements or specific derogations. However, these instruments may only be applied to punctual situations and cannot be used for repetitive transfers.

399. These options are also laid out in its Articles 33, III and forward:

> III — where the transfer is required for international legal cooperation between government intelligence, investigation and police bodies, in accordance with the international law instruments;
> IV — where the transfer is required for life protection or physical integrity of the data subject or any third party;
> V — where the supervisory authority authorizes such transfer;
> VI — where the transfer results in a commitment undertaken under an international cooperation agreement;
> VII — where the transfer is required for enforcement of a public policy or legal attribution of the public utility upon disclosure of the provisions of item I of the main provision of Article 23 of this Law;
> VIII — where the data subject has provided specific and highlighted consent for such transfer, with previous information on the international nature of the operation, clearly distinguishing it from any other purposes; or
> IX — where required to meet the hypotheses established in items II, V and VI of Article 7 of this Law.

400. The purpose of these tools is to ensure that all personal data that is transferred guards with itself the same standards of protection offered for processing occurring inside the scope of the LGPD.

§2. INTERNATIONAL DATA TRANSFER MECHANISMS

I. Appropriate Safeguards: Adequacy Decisions

401. An adequacy decision is when the ANPD accesses the level of protection that a third country or international organization offers and then decides, considering if the safeguards provided are adequate and compatible with Brazilian legislation.

402. When a third country or international organization is part of the National Authority Adequacy Decisions list, the transborder transfer may take place without the need to obtain any further authorization.

403. Once an adequacy decision is in place, data might be freely transferred from Brazil to a third country or organization, having the same procedure as if it was inside the territory.

404. Adequacy decisions are economically beneficial as it significantly lowers transaction costs for companies, opening new businesses and trade opportunities.

405. The proceedings adopted by the ANPD to assess the level of protection offered by a third country take into consideration six main elements described in Article 34 of the LGPD:

> I — the general and sectorial rules of the applicable law in the country of destination or international organization;
> II — the data nature;
> III — the compliance with the general principles of protection of personal data and rights of the data subjects established in this Law;
> IV — the adoption of security measures provided for by regulations;
> V — the existence of legal and institutional guarantees for compliance with personal data protection rights; and
> VI — any other specific circumstances concerning the transfer.

406. The first and most-time consuming step is the analysis of the rule of law and relevant legislation, especially the ones related to data protection.

407. The eventual existence of trade agreements with a third country does not guarantee the conceding of an adequacy decision, even though the country is an important trade partner. Privacy is not a commodity that can be traded; for this reason, the legislation and judicial regime of the third country must offer effective and properly enforceable data subject rights, guaranteeing the required essential equivalent level of protection.

408. In a globalized world where the Digital Single Market eliminates borders and connects people and businesses worldwide, having the authorization to allow the free flow of personal data with the most important economies, such as the EU, is an elementary competitive differential. Nowadays, the transfer of personal data happens on a massive scale, and businesses having restrictions to perform them will definitely suffer significant losses.

409. Despite the European approach to the matter, Araújo[96] points out that there are some relevant features that receive special attention and must hold a strong similarity with the GDPR provisions for the Commission to grant an Adequacy Decision, which are: Grant of rights applied to all data subjects irrespective of nationality/residence; Stronger consent requirements; Mandatory DPOs and mandatory DPIAs for certain types of processing; Data protection by design and by default; Direct liability and demonstrable accountability for processing agents; Data breach notifications; Representation of foreign controllers; Fines according to revenue; and last, DPAs must be settled, able to make decisions and issue sanctions, which might be judicially appealed and also must cooperate in international affairs.

410. The Brazilian Data Protection Authority has not issued any adequacy decision yet. However, in its updated Regulatory Agenda, published by Ordinance No 35,[97] Articles 33, 34 and 35 of the LGPD regarding international data transfers are planned to be regulated in 2023 if there is no delay again.

411. This means that, currently, this transfer mechanism cannot be used by a lack of specific regulation.

II. Appropriate Safeguards: Standard Contractual Clauses

412. SCCs are a set of contractual terms and conditions to be issued by the ANPD, in which the sender and receiver of cross-border data leaving the Brazilian territory have agreed on through contractual obligations.

413. SCCs allow transfers to be made between different companies, establishing rules through a contract and allowing the flow of data between controllers, joint controllers, processors, and sub-processors.

414. However, as adequacy decisions, SCCs have not been published yet by the ANPD.

96. A. Araújo, *The Right to Data Protection and the Commissions' Adequacy Decision*, 1 UNIO—EU Law Journal 77–93 (2015). Available at: doi:10.21814/unio.1.6. Accessed on Nov. 21, 2021.
97. National Data Protection Authority. Ordinance No. 35, of Nov. 08, 2022, makes the regulatory agenda for the 2023–2024 biennium public. Available at: https://www.gov.br/anpd/pt-br/assuntos/noticias/anpd-publica-agenda-regulatoria-2023-2024. Access on Jan. 24, 2023.

415. Miriam Wimmer, one of ANPD's directors, recently gave a speech[98] during the eleventh Brazilian Internet Forum, stating that standard contractual clauses will be the first transfer mechanism to be regulated:

> After conversations with other countries, it seemed interesting to us to start with the standard contractual clauses, because they are off-the-shelf mechanisms, which are fairly easy for large companies in their international contracts, without generating too much cost or time (…)
> (…) We had as a basis, in the matter of standard contractual clauses, the European ones, which are now quite complicated; and from New Zealand and Singapore, which are simpler; and it seemed to us that this is the best way to start, initially.

416. Given the above, SCCs will probably be the first tool to be published by the National Authority.

III. Appropriate Safeguards: Specific Contractual Clauses

417. Specific Contractual Clauses, which should not be confused with SCCs, are a set of clauses that might be individually submitted for approval by the ANPD regarding specific data transfers between transferor and transferee.

418. The approval process by the ANPD also has not started yet, as stated on its website:[99]

> "The procedures that will guide the actions of ANPD regarding the documents mentioned in Article 35 of Law No. 13.709, of August 14, 2018 (General Law on Personal Data Protection—LGPD).
> For this reason, activities relating to the definition of the content of standard contractual clauses or the verification of specific contractual clauses relating to the international transfer of personal data are not yet being carried out."

419. However, when the approval process starts to occur, ANPD might request additional information or steps to verify the processing operations included in the submitted contract (Article 35, § 2, of the LGPD).

420. Even though the approval process is not in course yet, this is currently the most used mechanism in Brazil.

---

98. Jose Norberto Flesch, Brasil começa modelo de remessa de dados com clausula padrão, diz ANPD. Available at: https://www.telesintese.com.br/brasil-comeca-modelo-de-remessa-de-dados-com-clausula-padrao-diz-anpd/. Access on Nov. 26, 2021.
99. ANPD. Canais de Atendimento, Agente de Tratamento, Transferência Internacional de Dados. Available at: https://www.gov.br/anpd/pt-br/canais_atendimento/agente-de-tratamento/transferencia-internacional-de-dados. Access on Nov. 28, 2021.

421. Brazil lives in a period of legal uncertainty since most of the mechanisms available for carrying out international transfers need previous approval or regulation by the ANPD.

422. Currently, by the letter of the law, only derogations or bilateral agreements would allow the licit international transfer of personal data, which are instruments destined for punctual circumstances, which is impracticable for companies.

423. This is the reason why Specific Contractual Clauses, based on the SCCs approved by the European Commission, are already in use, even though they have not been analyzed or approved yet. The recommendation is to submit these specific clauses for approval as soon as the approval process by ANPD starts.

IV. Appropriate Safeguards: Binding Corporate Rules

424. BCRs or Global Corporative Rules means personal data protection instruments, approved in accordance with the consistency mechanism, which are adhered to by a controller or processor set in the Brazilian territory for transfers of personal data to a controller or processor in one or more third countries within a group of undertakings or enterprises in a joint economic activity, including their employees.

425. This concept was imported into the General Protection Regulation since LGPD does not define specifically what the BCRs are or the proceedings to their adoption. However, once the Brazilian Legislation was mainly based on the GDPR, it is expected that the ANPD adopts the same criteria and procedures.

426. The definition and the procedure to adopt BCRs are described in Article 47[100] of the GDPR, which sets them as legally binding instruments which shall apply to and be enforced by every member concerned of a group of undertakings or enterprises engaged in a joint economic activity.

427. These binding provisions shall confer enforceable rights on data subjects regarding the processing of their personal data.

428. Organizations that operated on a worldwide basis needed more effective and less costly ways to legitimize their international data transfers; entering contractual arrangements for every subsidiary and its data transfers was impractical.

429. In 2003, the concept of BCRs was developed by European Data Protection Authorities to allow multinational corporations and groups of companies to make intraorganizational transfers of personal data across borders.[101]

---

100. Eduardo Ustaran, *European Data Protection Law and Practice* 504 (International Association of Privacy Professionals 2018).
101. *Ibid.*

430. These global sets of rules, based on Brazilian privacy standards, shall be drafted and followed voluntarily by multinational organizations, which are possible for approval by national regulators in accordance with their own legislation.

431. According to the GDPR, DPAs must approve a set of BCRs provided that it is legally binding and expressly confers enforceable rights on data subjects.

432. As it occurs with the Specific Contractual Clauses, ANPD might request additional information or steps to verify the processing operations included in the BCRs (Article 35, § 2, of the LGPD).

V. Seals, Certificates, and Codes of Conduct

433. Codes of Conduct[102] might be created by trade associations or other bodies that represent controllers or processors in consultation with relevant stakeholders and the public.

434. Using GDPR as a reference, the EDPB Guidelines 1/2019,[103] a non-exhaustive list of possible code owners, would include trade and representative associations, sectoral organizations, academic organizations and interest groups.

435. A draft of such codes must be sent to the ANPD for approval. The aim of these codes is to provide a voluntary tool that resolves data protection concerns in some areas, helping with its compliance for different sectors with its own particularities, as well as functioning as an international data transfer mechanism.

436. Approved certification mechanisms shall be established with the purpose of demonstrating compliance with the LGPD, allowing them to improve transparency with businesses and individuals. Certification schemes might be used for the purpose of demonstrating the existence of appropriate safeguards for international data transfers.

437. Certification proceedings shall be approved by the ANPD and can cover a specific issue or be more general. The authority might designate certification bodies to carry out the certification accreditation, which will remain under its supervision under the terms defined in the LGPD.

438. Once an accredited certification body has assessed and approved an organization, it will issue them with a certificate and a seal or mark relevant to that scheme.

---

102. ICO, Guide to the General Data Protection Regulation (GDPR): Codes of Conduct. Available at: https://ico.org.uk/for-organisations/guide-to-data-protection/guide-to-the-general-data-protection-regulation-gdpr/accountability-and-governance/codes-of-conduct/. Access on Dec. 1, 2021

103. EDPB, Guidelines 1/2019 on Codes of Conduct and Monitoring Bodies under Regulation 2016/679. Available at: https://edpb.europa.eu/sites/default/files/files/file1/edpb_guidelines_201901_v2.0_codesofconduct_en.pdf. Access on Dec. 1, 2021.

439. Certification and seal can lead to quickly assessing the level of data protection of a particular product, process or service, which provides transparency both for data subjects and for stakeholders.[104]

440. ANPD shall consider as requirements for the approval of such mechanisms the minimum conditions and guarantees for the transfer to comply with the rights, guarantees and principles of the LGPD (Article 35, § 1, of the LGPD).

441. There could also be financial benefits since the adherence of a business to such certifications, seals and codes of conduct is a fact that shall be considered by the ANPD whenever a fine under the LGPD must be imposed.

VI. Derogations and Bilateral Agreements

442. Derogations[105] cover situations where an adequacy decision or appropriate safeguards do not take place with the third country to which the transfer is being made; however, the risks to the data subjects are relatively small, or other interests override the data's subject right to privacy.

443. Data exports can be lawfully made under punctual circumstances, such as the explicit consent of the individual, where necessary for the performance of a contract or part of pre-contractual measures, as a legal obligation, when there is an international legal cooperation between government bodies, whenever necessary for establishing, exercising or defending legal claims, to protect vital interests, where the ANPD authorizes the specific transfer, where the transfer results in a commitment undertaken under an international cooperation agreement, or where the transfer is required for the enforcement of a public policy by the public administration.

444. The aforementioned transfer methods do not require prior approval or regulation by ANPD, which means they are all available for use immediately. However, most of them require previous international cooperation or agreements or are likely to be used in punctual and not repetitive transfers.

445. It is laborious and costly for processing agents to collect consent for each and every transfer where none of the other derogations are applicable since almost all data flows include international data transfers due to the use of different systems, such as e-mail and cloud services.

104. ICO, Guide to the General Data Protection Regulation (GDPR), Accountability and Governance, Certification. Available at: https://ico.org.uk/for-organisations/guide-to-data-protection/guide-to-the-general-data-protection-regulation-gdpr/accountability-and-governance/certification/. Access on Dec. 1, 2021.

105. Christopher Kuner, *Reality and Illusion in EU Data Transfer Regulation Post Schrems*, 18 German L.J. 881 (2017). Available at: https://ssrn.com/abstract=2732346 or http://dx.doi.org/10.2139/ssrn.2732346. Access on Dec. 1, 2021.

446. It is common sense that the LGPD came into force following technological developments, globalization, and the worldwide concern for privacy, centralizing and protecting the data subject.

447. Almost fully based on the GDPR, the legislators left some gaps to be explored and regulated by the National Authority. International data transfer is one of them.

448. Currently, between the transfer mechanisms made available by the LGPD, only some of them might be used before prior regulation or approval by the ANPD. This is a great obstacle for processing agents to keep their processing operations licit.

449. Alternative measures are being taken in order to suppress the gaps that have not been covered yet, such as the use of specific contractual clauses as the main mechanism to support data transfer, with submission to the ANPD only when the latter has the assessment and approval process open.

450. Legally this is not the best alternative; however, practically, it is the only one that works during ANPD inertia to keep the business functioning.

451. It is expected that ANPD will continue the regulation process that began in 2021 for the next biennium of 2023-2024, and with the regulation, there are high hopes from the market to end the legal uncertainty that arouses the theme.

Chapter 2. Transfers in the Context of International Agreements (For Example, Mutual Legal Assistance Treaties)

452. International data transfer is a very exciting theme with many questions and discussions, whether for academia, practitioners, or supervisory authorities. Narrowing this theme in the context of international agreements is an even bigger challenge. This chapter seeks to give a brief overview of the Brazilian situation according to the LGPD based on Article 33 (III) (VI) and Article 4 (III). Further, it offers an overview of the international cooperation under the ANPD developed so far.

453. International data transfer is a reality from which companies and organizations cannot run away. It brings several impacts to the rights of data subjects[106] and necessary due diligence to controllers and processors. It is also a topic that goes beyond the legal sphere and has deep connections with political and economic scenarios.

454. Before the Brazilian Data Protection Law (LGPD), this topic was already a concern addressed by Brazilian legislators. On April 23, 2014, the Brazilian Civil Rights Framework for the Internet (Marco Civil da Internet), Law No. 12.965/14, entered into force and brought the users' rights related to international data transfer in its Article 11.[107]

---

106. Christopher Kuner, *Reality and Illusion in EU Data Transfer Regulation Post Schrems*, 18(4) *German Law Journal* 881-918, 882 (2017). SSRN-id2732346.

107. SwissCam. LGPD: Authorization for International Transfer and Regulation by ANPD. Renata Armonia, Bruno Guilhem e Natália Dantas Fleury, Coimbra & Rhomberg Advogados. Available at: https://swisscam.com.br/en/publicacao/doing-business-in-brazil/33-brazilian-general-data-protection-law-lgpd/. Accessed on Dec. 22, 2021.

Art. 11. Any operation of collection, storage, storage and treatment of records, personal data or communications by connection providers and internet applications in which at least one of these acts occurs in national territory is subject to Brazilian law and must respect privacy rights, protection of personal data and confidentiality of private communications and records. §1° The above-mentioned provision applies to data collected in the national territory and the content of communications, provided that at least one of the terminals is located in Brazil.

§2° The above-mentioned provision applies even if the activities are carried out by a legal entity headquartered abroad, provided that it offers services to the Brazilian public or at least one member of the same economic group has an establishment in Brazil.

§3° The connection and internet application providers shall provide, in accordance with the regulations, information that allows verification of compliance with Brazilian legislation regarding the collection, safekeeping, storage or processing of data, as well as regarding respect of privacy and confidentiality of communications.

§4° Decree will regulate the procedure for investigating violations of the provisions of this article."

455. The Brazilian Civil Rights Framework for the Internet was the first legislation in Brazil regarding Internet governance, as there was no specific legislation in the country dealing with the subject until then.[108]

456. This reference gives an overview of the previous legislation before LGPD.

457. This chapter discusses international transfer in the context of international cooperation to secure the transfer of data as per Article 33 LGPD. It also brings some aspects of Article 4 (III) LGPD, which excludes the applicability of this law to the processing of personal data when it is done exclusively for purposes of public safety, national defense, state security, or activities of investigation and prosecution of criminal offenses.[109]

458. Sections III and VI and Article 4(III) bring different aspects of international transfer related to international cooperation, which are explained in the next subdivisions. Finally, this chapter approaches the actual status of international cooperation by the Brazilian Data Protection Authority (ANPD).

§1. International Data Transfer and International Cooperation

459. Having a safer data flow of personal data could be positive for Brazil's economy if regions such as the European Union or individual countries recognize that Brazil has a high level of data protection due to the implementation of mechanisms adopted after the LGPD. This would lead countries to recognize and approve of a free flow of personal data between them and Brazil. Moreover, there is also a social benefit when Brazil earns recognition as a nation with a high level of intimacy protection. The opposite is also true, and Article 33 LGPD can also be used to give adequacy recognition to a specific country or region and make the personal data flow easier. This could be done via an international agreement.[110]

460. Seeking to create a better understanding of the provisions related to international data transfer in LGPD and when its use is permitted, here follows Article 33:

---

108. SwissCam Brasil 33. Brazilian General Data Protection Law (LGPD). Available at: https://swisscam.com.br/en/publicacao/doing-business-in-brazil/33-brazilian-general-data-protection-law-lgpd/ International Data Transfer Renata Armonia, Bruno Guilhem e Natália Dantas. Access on Dec. 22, 2021.

109. Rennó Penteado Sampaio Advogados. Translation by Ronaldo Lemos, Natalia Langenegger, Juliana Pacetta Ruiz, Sofia Lima Franco, Andréa Guimarães Gobbato, Daniel Douek, Ramon Alberto dos Santos and Rafael A. Ferreira Zanatta. As amended by Law no. 13,583, after congressional override of presidential vetoes. This translation was based on an initial version by Monica Hruby (www.mhruby.com). Available at: https://iapp.org/media/pdf/resource_center/Brazilian_General_Data_Protection_Law.pdf. Access on Dec. 21, 2021.

110. Mario Viola, *Transferência de Dados entre Europa e Brasil: Análise da Adequação da Legislação Brasileira*1–22 (ITS 2019).

Art. 33. International transfer of personal data is only allowed in the following cases:

I — to countries or international organizations that provide a degree of personal data protection adequate to that foreseen in this Law;
II — when the controller offers and proves guarantees of compliance with the principles, the subject's rights and the data protection regime provided in this Law, in the form of:
(a) specific contractual clauses for a given transfer;
b) standard contractual clauses
c) global corporate standards;
d) seals, certificates and codes of conduct regularly issued;
III — when the transfer is necessary for international legal cooperation between public intelligence, investigative and prosecutorial agencies, in accordance with the instruments of international law;
IV — when the transfer is necessary to protect the life or physical safety of the subject or of a third party;
V — when the national authority authorizes the transfer;
VI — when the transfer results from a commitment assumed in an international cooperation agreement;
VII — when the transfer is necessary for the execution of a public policy or legal attribution of the public service, with publicity being given under the terms of item I in the caput of art. 23 of this Law;
VIII — when the subject has provided his specific and detached consent to the transfer, with prior information on the international character of the operation, clearly distinguishing it from other purposes; or
IX — when necessary to meet the hypotheses foreseen in items II, V, and VI of art. 7 of this Law.
(...)

461. The article above is objective and sets limits to personal data international transfer, establishing that the only possibilities that authorize a transfer to happen are the above-mentioned and any other option not being feasible.

462. As a general understanding, Article 33 (III) LGPD allows an international transfer of data when there is the same level of adequacy towards data protection between public intelligence and investigative and prosecutorial agencies, in accordance with the instruments of international law. This mechanism is important when there is an investigation of digital crimes, for example. Those crimes can be decentralized and spread through different jurisdictions. Therefore, international cooperation is needed in order to find evidence and proof of the respective crime in a timely manner.[111] This being said, Article 4 (III) LGPD excludes the applicability of LGPD for security or investigations of criminal offenses. This decision is similar to the

111. Vieira Jusbrasil, Victor. LGPD Transferencia internacional de dados. Available at: https://vieiravictor.jusbrasil.com.br/artigos/726523659/lei-geral-de-protecao-de-dados-transferencia-internacional-de-dados-pessoais. Access on Dec. 26, 2021.

European model, which has the Law Enforcement Directive (EU) 2016/680 (LED) as a specific regime to be followed by the authorities. Currently, the Brazilian legislator aims to approve the Criminal LGPD draft bill. This bill is under discussion, but as pointed out by Mario Viola, it will allow the exchange of information in the context of police and legal cooperation even without an adequacy decision in place, the Budapest Convention, or mutual legal assistance.[112] These two last mechanisms are so far used in order to exchange information related to criminal law. They were established via international cooperation. Regarding Mutual Legal Assistance Treaties (MLATs), Brazil has several MLATs in place. However, this mechanism is not always optimal, and the federation of associations of information technology companies are challenged in the Federal Supreme Court action of constitutionality n. 51 related to an MLAT within the U.S. There are different complaints about MLATs, such as the long period to receive an answer (around eighteen months), and quite often, the requirements are done directly with the respective foreign company instead of MLATs.[113]

463. This being said, the Criminal LGPD draft bill aims to guarantee efficiency, protection of personal data, and the fundamental rights of data subjects. To achieve such goals, this draft bill clearly establishes the scope of its application and sets a list of principles assuring that its provisions shall be aligned with human rights, free personality development, freedom of speech, presumption of innocence and others.

464. Due to the increase of subject data protection in the field of public security, some barriers may arise to the day-a-day work of the police forces since the range of discretionary investigation actions would be diminished. That is a side effect of the draft bill, which should be faced through a proportionality principle lens in order to balance the use of international transfer for the development of public security while it also secures the privacy and data protection of the subjects. Article 33 (VI) LGPD reinforces the obligation to perform the international data transfer due to international cooperation. In fact, those sections from Article 33 LGPD allow Brazil to enter international cooperation, whether bilateral or multilateral, to make the flow of personal data less bureaucratic and less expensive for companies. In 2021, Brazil joined the Budapest Convention, which will help speed up access to electronic evidence under foreigners' jurisdiction.

§2. International Cooperation under the ANPD

465. The ANPD has a Regulatory Agenda for the period of 2021–2022, which contains international data transfer as one of the items to be implemented via

112. Mario Viola, *Transferência de Dados entre Europa e Brasil: Análise da Adequação da Legislação Brasileira* 9 (ITS November 2019).
113. Mario Viola & Leonardo Heringer & Celina Carvalho, Relatorio-Transferencia-de-dados-pessoais.pdf 16 (ITS Instituto de Tecnologia & Sociedade do Rio 2021).

resolution during the second phase.[114] Until the end of December 2021, the agency did not issue guidance on international data transfer.[115] However, in July 2021, during her participation in the eleventh Internet Forum in Brazil, ANPD Director Miriam Wimmer said:

> After conversations with other countries, it seemed interesting to us to start with the standard contractual clauses, since they are off-the-shelf mechanisms and somewhat convenient for large companies in their international contracts, without generating too much cost or time. We had as a basis, regarding standard contractual clauses, the European models, which are now quite complicated; those from New Zealand and Singapore seem simpler; initially, we found that this is the best path.[116]

466. This statement reflects that the ANPD is observing data protection mechanisms outside Europe. Even if the LGPD has similarities with the GDPR, the agency demonstrates that it is observing the international best practices in order to choose the simpler mechanism, which will generate less costs for the Brazilian industries.

467. Nevertheless, it is worth mentioning that while the gap still exists, the Brazilian academia and practitioners are using the European experience, e.g., SCC, BCRs and DPA as a model to adapt to the Brazilian reality.

I. The ANPD Strategic Plan 2021–2023

468. In its strategic plan, its vision is to become a national and international reference in Personal Data Protection. The ANPD wants to promote relationships with society and with partners.[117] Further, the agency will also manage institutional and international relations.[118]

469. The agency also defines as one of its goals the promotion of specific technical cooperation mechanisms that allow the exchange of knowledge and

114. ANDP. Nota Técnica No. 37/2021/CGN/ANPD. Relatório de Acompanhamento e Execução da Agenda Regulatória para o biênio 2021–2022—2/2021. Available at: https://www.gov.br/anpd/pt-br/assuntos/sei_00261-000027_2021_64.pdf. Access on Dec. 20, 2021.
115. ANDP. Agente de Tratamento. Available at: https://www.gov.br/anpd/pt-br/canais_atendimento/agente-de-tratamento/transferencia-internacional-de-dados. Access Dec. 20, 2021.
116. Telesintese. Brasil começa modelo de remessa de dados com cláusula padrão, diz anpd. Available at: https://www.telesintese.com.br/brasil-comeca-modelo-de-remessa-de-dados-com-clausula-padrao-diz-anpd/. Access on Dec. 20, 2021.
117. ANPD. Planejamento estratégico. Available at: https://www.gov.br/anpd/pt-br/documentos-e-publicacoes/planejamento-estrategico/planejamento-estrategico-2021-2023.pdf. Access on Dec. 20, 2021.
118. ANPD. Proposta de Cadeia de Valor e Macroprocessos da ANPD. Available at: https://www.gov.br/anpd/pt-br/acesso-a-informacao/transparencia-e-prestacao-de-contas-1/transparencia-e-prestacao-de-contas-2021/cadeia_de_valor_anpd___final.pdf. Accessed on Dec. 20, 2021.

experiences, besides identifying the best practices in the field of personal data protection.[119]

470. During its first year of existence, the ANPD agency signed a memorandum of understanding with the Spanish Data Protection Agency (AEPD). This was the first cooperation agreement signed by ANPD and another supervisory authority to achieve and disseminate the culture of personal data protection.[120] This is in accordance with Article 55-J (IX) LGPD: (..) IX—to promote cooperation initiatives with data protection authorities of other countries of international or transnational nature.

471. To make this international cooperation a reality, ANPD adhered as a member of the Ibero-American Data Protection network "Red Iberoamericana de Protección de Datos" (RIPD).

472. RIPD is a forum to discuss and develop the best practices in order to protect personal data surrounding Latin America.[121]

473. The Ibero-American States will be able to adopt international cooperation mechanisms that facilitate the application of the corresponding national legislation in the matter, which may include, in an enunciative but non-limiting manner: (a) the establishment of mechanisms that make it possible to reinforce assistance and international cooperation in the application of the respective national legislation in the matter; (b) assistance among control authorities through notification and remission of complaints, assistance in investigations and exchange of information; and (c) the adoption of mechanisms aimed at the knowledge and exchange of best practices and experiences in the field of personal data protection, including those relating to conflicts of jurisdiction with third countries.[122]

474. The opportunity to be part of the RIPD network will add a lot of value to the new supervisory authority in Brazil, mainly to strengthen the exchange among supervisory authorities in the region. The network includes Argentina and Uruguay,

---

119. ANDP. Memorando de Entendimento. Available at: https://www.gov.br/anpd/pt-br/assuntos/noticias/anpd-assina-memorando-de-entendimento-com-a-agencia-espanhola-de-protecao-de-dados. Access on Dec. 23, 2021.
120. ANDP. ANPD assina Memorando de Entendimento com a Agência Espanhola de Proteção de Dados. Available at: https://www.gov.br/anpd/pt-br/assuntos/noticias/anpd-assina-memorando-de-entendimento-com-a-agencia-espanhola-de-protecao-de-dados. Access on Dec. 25, 2021.
121. ANDP. ANPD torna-se membro da Rede Ibero-Americana de proteção de dados. Available at: https://www.gov.br/anpd/pt-br/assuntos/noticias/anpd-torna-se-membro-da-rede-ibero-americana-de-protecao-de-dados. Access on Dec. 26, 2021.
122. *Ibid.* https://www.gov.br/anpd/pt-br/assuntos/noticias/mou-anpd-aepd-pt.pdf: "Os Estados Ibero-Americanos poderão adotar mecanismos de cooperação internacional que facilitem a aplicação das legislações nacionais correspondentes na matéria, os quais poderão compreender, de maneira enunciativa mas não limitativa: (a) O estabelecimento de mecanismos que permitam reforçar a assistência e a cooperação internacional na aplicação das respectivas legislações nacionais na matéria; (b) A assistência entre as autoridades de controle através da notificação e remissão de reclamações, assistência em investigações e intercâmbio de informação; e (c) A adoção de mecanismos voltados para o conhecimento e intercâmbio das melhores práticas e experiências em matéria de proteção de dados pessoais, inclusive no relativo a conflitos de jurisdição com terceiros países."

and both have the recognition of the European Commission as countries with an adequacy level of protection for the purposes of international data transfer with the European Union. Further, the network also comprises important organizations such as the European Data Protection Supervisor (EDPS), the Organization of American States (OAS) and the Council of Europe as observers.

475. The LGPD does not answer all the questions while dealing with international data transfer. However, the law gives mechanisms to be developed and articulated by the ANPD and Brazilian legislators. The LGPD and the Criminal LGPD draft bill also generate discussions on the mechanisms used so far when personal data are transferred in different contexts.

476. The work performed so far by the ANPD demonstrates that the agency wants to get into the international route of data protection discussions. The path is certainly long. In the meantime, practitioners, academia, and industry that process personal data and have international data transfer in their daily business will keep using the European model, e.g., as a reference to keep doing their business.

Part VIII. Enforcement

Chapter 1. Supervisory Authorities

477. The ANPD was created through Law 13.853/2019. The authority has its own powers and responsibilities, so it is very important to understand its origin and scope of action.

478. As previously mentioned, the LGPD was sanctioned in 2018; however, the law was approved with some vetoes by President Michel Temer. The most relevant veto was the veto on the creation of the ANPD.

479. This did not prevent the creation of authority further on, but the veto had its reason to exist within the Brazilian legal system. ANPD was conceived to act as the LGPD's supervisory body, working as a state agency, responsible for supervising compliance with the standard and applying applicable sanctions in situations of noncompliance with the law.

480. In detail, the ANPD had its creation vetoed during the sanction of the LGPD because, according to the Brazilian Constitution, the creation of a supervisory body must be done through the initiative of the executive power and cannot happen by the initiative of the legislative power—as it was the case with the creation of ANPD by Law 13.709/2018.

481. This constitutional understanding is indicated by Article 37, XIX of the Federal Constitution,[123] whose content highlights that regulatory agencies have characteristics equivalent to those of autarchies and, therefore, must be created by initiatives of the Executive.

482. Therefore, the veto only concerned the "initiative vice" resulting from the creation of the ANPD and not the creation of the authority itself, which was seen as essential for the Brazilian legal system. For this reason, Temer pledged to create the ANPD until the end of his government. What happened at the end of his term of office through Provisional Measure No. 869 of December 27, 2018, which was later converted into Law No. 13.853 of July 8, 2019?

123. XIX—only a specific law may create an autarchy and authorize the establishment of a public company, a mixed-capital company and a foundation, with the complementary law being responsible, in the latter case, for defining the areas of its performance.

483. In general terms, it is stated that the ANPD was created with the aim of bringing more security and stability to the application of the General Data Protection Law.

484. Another relevant feature of the creation of ANPD is that of guaranteeing the limits of application of the LGPD, that is, of acting as a regulator of the application of the rules for the protection of personal data in Brazil. This can be noticed since, in several articles of the LGPD, it is possible to find the forecast of future regulation of certain institutes or devices by ANPD.

485. This emphasis is important because this regulatory role drives the adaptation of the LGPD's normative understanding to the socioeconomic reality of Brazil, a fact that ensures that the law is adopted by the institutions that carry out data processing in the country.

486. In this sense, it can be said that ANPD has a centralizing function for the applicable standards of the LGPD. Because of this, there is a huge responsibility for those appointed to positions within the Authority, with this responsibility being more impactful on those appointed in the first term of ANPD, as they are responsible for creating the legal framework for the protection of personal data in the country.[124]

487. It is also noteworthy that ANPD works as a connector between various areas of interest, as it also centralizes the interest of the:

- Recipients: that use the body as a reference entity in situations involving the violation of their ownership rights.
- Private entities: that observe and follow the structures established by the authority, thus managing to act with more assertiveness in the search for conformity.
- Public entities: as it concentrates the inspection of matters involving the protection of personal data.[125]

488. Such centralization can also be observed from the perspective of other institutions since other regulatory and supervisory authorities in the country, as well as the three Executive, Legislative and Judiciary branches, "which should continue to understand the subject of the dynamics of personal data in a non-conforming context only national but mainly international so that Brazil knows how to position itself in the global digital market."[126]

---

124. Decree No. 10.474, of Aug. 26, 2020 created ANPD's regimental structure and demonstrative table of positions.
125. It is necessary to point out that ANPD is not the only institution that can decide on data protection matters, as: "Art. 52 [...] § 2 The provisions of this article do not replace the application of administrative, civil or criminal sanctions defined in Law No. 8.078, of September 11, 1990, and in specific legislation."
126. Patricia Peck Pinheiro, *Personal Data Protection: Comments on Law n. 13.709/2018* 57 (Editora SaraivaJur 3d ed. 2021).

489. In this sense, the ANPD is very important, as it acts as an inspector and regulator of the application of the LGPD in the Brazilian scenario. GDPR's international experience, for example.

490. The GDPR detailed the appropriate parameters regarding the conduct and compliance procedures in its Articles 40 to 43; the LGPD was quite general on the subject in its Articles 50 and 51:

> Art. 50. The controllers and operators, within the scope of their competences, through the processing of personal data, individually or through associations, may formulate rules of good practices and governance that establish the conditions of organization, the operating regime, the procedures, including complaints and petitions from holders, security rules, technical standards, specific obligations for the various parties involved in the processing, educational actions, internal mechanisms for supervision and risk mitigation, and other aspects related to data processing personal.
> § 1 When establishing rules of good practice, the controller and the operator shall take into account, in relation to the processing and the data, the nature, scope, purpose and probability and severity of risks and benefits arising from data processing of the holder.
> § 2 In the application of the principles indicated in items VII and VIII of the main section of Article 6 of this Law, the controller, subject to the structure, scale and volume of its operations, as well as the sensitivity of the processed data and the probability and severity of damage to data subjects, may:
>
> I — implement a privacy governance program that, at a minimum:
> a) demonstrates the controller's commitment to adopting internal processes and policies that ensure comprehensive compliance with standards and good practices relating to the protection of personal data;
> b) is applicable to the entire set of personal data under its control, regardless of the way in which it was collected;
> c) is adapted to the structure, scale and volume of its operations, as well as the sensitivity of the data processed;
> d) establish adequate policies and safeguards based on a systematic assessment process of impacts and risks to privacy;
> e) has the objective of establishing a relationship of trust with the titleholder, through transparent action and ensuring mechanisms for the participation of the titleholder;
> f) is integrated into its general governance structure and establishes and applies internal and external supervisory mechanisms;
> g) have incident response and remediation plans; and
> h) is constantly updated based on information obtained from continuous monitoring and periodic evaluations;
>
> II — demonstrate the effectiveness of its privacy governance program when appropriate and, in particular, at the request of the national

authority or other entity responsible for promoting compliance with good practices or codes of conduct, which independently promote the compliance with this Law.

§ 3 The rules of good practice and governance must be published and updated periodically and may be recognized and disseminated by the national authority.
Art. 51. The national authority will encourage the adoption of technical standards that facilitate control by the holders of their personal data.

491. Because of this, ANPD's regulatory work is so relevant. And it has been more intense, as seen in the schedule of activities published by the authority through Ordinance No. 11, January 27, 2021, better explained later.

492. In February 2021, ANPD published its "Strategic Planning 2021–2023," in which it points out its values:

- Ethic
- Transparency
- Integrity
- Impartiality
- Efficiency
- Responsibility.

493. Aspects of strategic relevance for Brazil, considering that ensuring a good level of personal data protection is an indicator of legal security and, consequently, a good economic indicator for countries.

494. This experience is observed in other countries, considering that the good performance of national authorities for the protection of personal data has been observed to measure security in the analysis of economic risk.[127,128]

495. According to the International Association of Privacy Professionals (IAPP), there are around 150 DPAs spread all over the world, and different approaches can be observed in the performance of these authorities:

(1) authorities with an orientation/inspection; and
(2) authorities with a punitive/collective character.

127. Samuel G. Goldberg, Garrett A. Johnson & Scott K. Shriver, *Regulating Privacy Online: An Economic Evaluation of the GDPR*. Marketing Science Institute Working Paper Series, Report No. 21-110, 2021.
128. IAPP. Data Protection Authority. 2020.

496. In this regard, it is noted that some authorities are open to answering public queries, working with the representative entities of the sectors, or even imposing less aggressive sanctions with an educational function, while other authorities are more punitive.[129]

497. Regardless of the authorities' action strategy, it can be noted that their work has influenced the behavior of institutions so that privacy and the protection of personal data are increasingly part of the routine of mandatory activities of public and private.

498. It is also pointed out that, according to the ICO, there are four pillars that guide the work of authorities in the protection of personal data, namely:

(a) ensuring the enforcement of privacy and data protection regulations;
(b) supervision, auditing and advising institutions that process personal data;
(c) educational guidance on best practices in personal data protection and privacy; and
(d) the follow-up and monitoring of the treatments that are carried out by the institutions.

499. It is also noteworthy that the Brazilian ANPD is also permeated by this vision since, in 2021, ANPD presented a very varied agenda, carrying out activities in all these pillars.

129. On the website https://www.enforcementtracker.com/ it is possible to monitor the application of sanctions in countries regulated by the GDPR and observe these trends.

Chapter 2. Composition

500. ANPD is made up of six government branches, including: (1) the Board of Directors; (2) the National Council for the Protection of Personal Data and Privacy; (3) Internal Affairs; (4) the Ombudsman; (5) own legal advisory body; and (6) administrative units and specialized units.

501. The LGPD reserves the articles from 55-A to 55-K for ANPD's composition matter, and each of these devices brings relevant information about the ANPD's structure and performance.

502. Article 55-A, § 1 of the LGPD, provides notes on the legal nature of the ANPD and is transitory since the authority was created as an entity linked to the Presidency of the Republic.

503. After two years, ANPD is transformed into an autarchy through the presentation of a proposal in this regard on the initiative of the Executive Power:

> Article 55-A. The National Data Protection Authority (ANPD), a federal public administration body, member of the Presidency of the Republic, was created without any increase in expenditure.
> § 1 The legal nature of ANPD is transitory and may be transformed by the Executive Branch into an indirect federal public administration entity, subject to a special autarchic regime and linked to the Presidency of the Republic.
> § 2 The assessment regarding the transformation provided for in § 1 of this article must take place within 2 (two) years from the date of entry into force of the ANPD regimental structure.
> § 3 The provision of positions and functions necessary for the creation and performance of ANPD is subject to express physical and financial authorization in the annual budget law and permission in the budget guidelines law[130]

504. During the creation of ANPD, the creation of the institution was analyzed along the lines of a regulatory agency, such as in countries like Portugal and France. Brazil, however, opted for the model of a public administration body.

505. It is also noteworthy that there are other countries that adopt a model similar to that implemented in Brazil, as is the case in England, given that the ICO has a very similar legal nature to the ANPD since the ICO is a public body with an obligation to report to the English Parliament and, at the same time, does not constitute its own department/folder. Anyway, the LGPD foresees the modification of this model, with the objective of bringing more independence and guaranteeing the authority's autonomy of action.

506. On the composition of ANPD, indicated in Article 55-C of the LGPD and which provides:

130. Brazil. Law 13.709 of Aug. 14, 2018, 2018.

Article 55-C. ANPD is composed of:

I — Board of Directors, highest governing body
II — National Council for the Protection of Personal Data and Privacy;
III — Internal Affairs;
IV — Ombudsman;
V — its own legal advisory body; and
VI — administrative units and specialized units necessary for the application of the provisions of this Law[131]

507. The Board of Directors is composed of five members, appointed by the Presidency of the Republic and with terms of office of four years, as per Article 55-D of the LGPD. The LGPD also points out that "art. 55-D [...] § 4 The terms of office of the first appointed members of the Board of Directors shall be 2 (two), 3 (three), 4 (four), 5 (five) and 6 (six) years, as established in the act of appointment."

508. The Board of Directors is the highest governing body of the Authority.

509. The National Council for Data Protection and Privacy is composed of twenty-three representatives, distributed as follows:

Article 58-A. The National Council for the Protection of Personal Data and Privacy will be composed of 23 (twenty-three) representatives, holders and alternates, from the following bodies:

I — 5 (five) of the Federal Executive Branch;
II — 1 (one) from the Federal Senate;
III — 1 (one) from the Chamber of Deputies;
IV — 1 (one) from the National Council of Justice;
V — 1 (one) from the National Council of the Public Ministry;
VI — 1 (one) of the Internet Steering Committee in Brazil;
VII — 3 (three) from civil society entities with activities related to the protection of personal data;
VIII — 3 (three) from scientific, technological and innovation institutions;
IX — 3 (three) from union confederations representing the economic categories of the productive sector;
X — 2 (two) from entities representing the business sector related to the area of processing personal data; and
XI — 2 (two) of entities representing the labor sector[132]

Art. 58-A, § 3, I and II of the LGPD, points out that the representatives of the National Council are appointed in the form of a regulation and have a term of office of 2 years, renewable for up to 1 year.

131. Brazil. Law 13.709 of Aug. 14, 2018, 2018.
132. *Ibid.*

510. The other bodies that make up the ANPD do not have their structure provided for in the law.

Chapter 3. Competence, Tasks, and Powers

511. ANPD is endowed with the competence to inspect, regulate, and apply the sanctions provided for in the LGPD and therefore has an extensive list of activities and possibilities for action.

512. ANPD has exclusive competence to apply the sanctions provided for in the LGPD, as highlighted in Article 55-k:

> Article 55-K. The application of the sanctions provided for in this Law is exclusively the responsibility of ANPD, and its powers will prevail, with regard to the protection of personal data, over the related powers of other entities or bodies of public administration.
>
> Single paragraph. ANPD will articulate its activities with other bodies and entities with sanctioning and regulatory powers related to the subject of personal data protection and will be the central body for interpreting this Law and establishing rules and guidelines for its implementation.[133]

513. Furthermore, the authority has the power to centralize the understanding and create the necessary guidelines for the application of the LGPD, as previously pointed out.

514. Important to note that ANPD's composition was created so that the authority would be able to act in all its powers, which are listed in Article 55-J of the LGPD:

> Article 55-J. It is incumbent upon ANPD:
>
> I — ensure the protection of personal data, under the terms of legislation;
> II — ensure the observance of commercial and industrial secrets, observing the protection of personal data and the confidentiality of information when protected by law or when the breach of confidentiality violates the foundations of Article 2 of this Law;
> III — prepare guidelines for the National Policy for the Protection of Personal Data and Privacy;
> IV — inspect and apply sanctions in the event of data processing carried out in breach of the law, through an administrative process that ensures the adversary system, full defense and the right to appeal;
> V — to consider petitions from the holder against the controller after the holder has proven the presentation of a claim to the controller that has not been resolved within the period established by regulation;
> VI — promote in the population the knowledge of the norms and public policies on the protection of personal data and security measures

133. *Ibid.*

VII — promote and prepare studies on national and international practices for the protection of personal data and privacy;

VIII — to encourage the adoption of standards for services and products that facilitate the exercise of control by the holders of their personal data, which must take into account the specificities of the activities and the size of those responsible;

IX — promote cooperation actions with personal data protection authorities from other countries, of an international or transnational nature;

X — to provide for forms of publicity for the processing of personal data, respecting commercial and industrial secrets;

XI — request, at any time, public authorities that carry out personal data processing operations to provide specific information on the scope, nature of the data and other details of the processing carried out, with the possibility of issuing a complementary technical opinion to ensure the compliance with this Law;

XII — prepare annual management reports about its activities;

XIII — edit regulations and procedures on the protection of personal data and privacy, as well as on impact reports on the protection of personal data for cases in which the treatment represents a high risk to guarantee the general principles of personal data protection provided for in this Law;

XIV — listen to treatment agents and society in matters of relevant interest and report on their activities and planning;

XV — collect and apply its revenues and publish, in the management report referred to in item XII of the caput of this article, the details of its revenues and expenses;

XVI — carry out audits, or determine their performance, within the scope of the inspection activity referred to in item IV and with due observance of the provisions of item II of the caput of this article, on the processing of personal data carried out by the processing agents, including the public power;

XVII — enter into, at any time, a commitment with processing agents to eliminate irregularities, legal uncertainty or contentious situations in the context of administrative proceedings, in accordance with the provisions of Decree-Law No. 4,657, of September 4, 1942;

XVIII — edit simplified and differentiated rules, guidelines and procedures, including with regard to deadlines, so that micro and small businesses, as well as business initiatives of an incremental or disruptive nature that declare themselves startups or innovation companies, can adapt to this Law;

XIX — to ensure that the processing of elderly data is carried out in a simple, clear, accessible and suitable way for their understanding, under the terms of this Law and Law No. 10,741, of October 1, 2003 (Statute of the Elderly);

XX — resolve, in the administrative sphere, in a terminative nature, on the interpretation of this Law, its powers and omissions;

XXI — communicate to the competent authorities the criminal offenses of which it becomes aware;
XXII — notify the internal control bodies of non-compliance with the provisions of this Law by bodies and entities of the federal public administration;
XXIII — liaise with public regulatory authorities to exercise their powers in specific sectors of economic and governmental activities subject to regulation; and
XXIV — implement simplified mechanisms, including by electronic means, for the registration of complaints about the processing of personal data in non-compliance with this Law.

§ 1 When imposing administrative constraints on the processing of personal data by a private processing agent, whether they are limits, charges or constraints, ANPD must observe[134]

515. Another activity that is within the ANPD's competence is to make the application of the LGPD closer to reality and, thus, more effective, both from the perspective of processing agents, data subjects and also institutions linked to the Government, such as the Public Ministry or the Consumer Regulation body (Procon and Idec), for example, as provided throughout the text of Article 55-J of the LGPD.

516. It is still observed that since ANPD has the "mission of ensuring the correct observance of the General Data Protection Law (LGPD) in Brazil,"[135] its first year of operation has been productive.

517. During this first year, efforts had to be allocated simultaneously between the structuring and consolidation of the body, which ranged from basic tasks such as finding a suitable physical space through raising financial and material resources and expanding the staff and their training in related technical matters, at the same time that inspection and regulation actions were being established and strengthened.

518. As a result, 15 Deliberative Circuits, published 17 Ordinances, signed 4 Technical Cooperation Agreements, completed 100% of the first phase of the Regulatory Agenda, and 6 educational materials, including Guides, Booklets, and Issues, have already been published by ANPD, with partners, and Articles. Concurrently with the activities, ANPD members also participated in 313 external events, in addition to the use of social networks and other communication tools to disseminate knowledge and content. There were also 7 consultations with society, including

134. *Ibid.*
135. National Personal Data Protection Authority. *National Authority for the Protection of Personal Data (ANPD) Completes 1 Year* (2021).

subsidy-taking, consultations and public hearings, with more than 3,000 written contributions in the Public Consultations and about 160 contributions in the Subsidy Takings carried out.[136]

519. ANPD's role is essential to guarantee the full application of the LGPD since through an institution with supervisory and regulatory powers, the chances that the law will be implemented in the routine of Brazilian citizens increase.

520. ANPD divides its regulatory projects into three central phases that are expected to be implemented within two years. Each of the phases has a period of operation according to the schedule below:

- Phase 1 (in up to a year): Publish its bylaws, Publish the 2021–2023 strategic planning, Create a differentiated regulation for micro and small companies (Article 55-J/LGPD), Define its own regulation on sanctions (Article 53/LGPD), Establish the criteria minimums on the reporting procedure (deadline, form and form of data submission) (Article 48/LGPD), Editing regulations and procedures on data protection and privacy and impact reporting (Article 55J, XIII/LGPD).
- Phase 2 (between one year and six months): The establishment of complementary rules on definitions and attributions of the data manager (Article 43, §3°/LGPD), Regulate Articles 33, 34 and 35 of the LGPD, which provides for the international transfer of data.
- Phase 3 (within two years): Regulate other aspects of the rights of holders of personal data and publish a guidance document on the legal bases and hypotheses for data processing described in Article 7 of the LGPD.

521. The three phases seek to address the central points of ANPD's activities, so important in the first term of office of the bodies. Although not all aspects of the ANPD's guidelines and understandings have yet been defined, the three phases demonstrate organization and planning by the authority, indicating a good path for its consolidation.

136. *Ibid.*

Chapter 4. Remedies

522. LGPD points out possibilities of remedies that could be used by the data subjects to the National Authority in certain cases, besides the possibility of the ANPD demand on how the processing of personal data is being held by the agents of processing.

523. One of the rights of the data subject imposed by the Brazilian data protection law refers to its possibility of filing a claim about the processing of their data to ANPD (Article 18, IX, §1º).

524. This right is provided not only by the LGPD but also by the Brazilian Constitution (Article 5º, XXXIV).

525. As it is understood, it is a right that every citizen holds to give them the possibility to claim any situation that might have caused harm or that breaks rights. With the data protection law, it comes to a specific case, guaranteed that, due to the specificity of the theme, it is met by the responsible body (Article 55-J, V).

526. Besides the power of the citizens that can be exerted, the ANPD can also demand from processing agents the DPIA (Article 38); they can audit these agents (Article 20, §2º) and other demands; nonetheless, all of them are based on the principles of the LGPD.

Chapter 5. Liabilities

527. As pointed out before in Part V, it is clear the liabilities defined by the processing agents, each one having its own demands to be accomplished while processing personal data. Besides, when it comes to ANPD's liability, although it seems to be an independent body, it is still linked to direct public administration.

528. As foreseen by the OECD, regulators should be independent in their activities, especially when it comes to data protection, being free of any interference, political or economic.

529. When it comes to Brazil's regulator (ANPD), their role is still bonded to the direct public administration. It has some institutional characteristics that give it greater independence, such as technical and decision-making autonomy and the fixed term of office of the Directors.

Chapter 6. Penalties

530. There are several sanctions to be implemented by ANPD, in which way the imputation of a penalty varies according to the damage caused, recurrence, context, etc.

531. The LGPD only provides for the imputation of administrative penalties, which makes sense since the law provided that only the ANPD is the competent body to impose legal sanctions on data protection.

532. This does not mean that other bodies cannot impose possible criminal, civil, or other administrative penalties when noncompliance with data protection obligations occurs.

533. It only means that, regarding the sanctions brought by the LGPD, the only body competent is the ANPD.

534. The sanctions applied due to the violation of the obligations and duties imposed by the legislation are explored by the LGPD in chapter VIII, which deals with administrative sanctions.

535. According to Article 52 list, there is a comprehensive list of penalties applicable to offending agents in the data processing activity:

> Art. 52. Data processing agents, due to infringements committed to the rules provided for in this Law, are subject to the following administrative sanctions applicable by the national authority:
>
> I — warning, indicating the deadline for taking corrective measures;
> II — simple fine, of up to 2% (two percent) of the revenue of a legal entity governed by private law, group or conglomerate in Brazil in its last fiscal year, excluding taxes, limited in total to R$ 50,000,000.00 (fifty million reais) per infraction;
> III — daily fine, observing the total limit referred to in item II;
> IV — publicizing the infringement after its occurrence has been duly investigated and confirmed;
> V — blocking of the personal data to which the infringement refers until its regularization;
> VI — deletion of personal data to which the infringement refers;
> VII — (VETOED);
> VIII — (VETOED);
> IX — (VETOED).
> X — (VETOED);
> XI — (VETOED);

X — partial suspension of the functioning of the database to which the infringement refers for a maximum period of 6 (six) months, extendable for an equal period, until the regularization of the processing activity by the controller;

XI — suspension of the exercise of the activity of processing personal data to which the infringement refers for a maximum period of 6 (six) months, extendable for an equal period;

XII — partial or total prohibition of the exercise of activities related to data processing.[137]

536. It is also observed that the LGPD determines that sanctions will be applied through an administrative procedure that respects basic procedural rights, such as full defense, and the extent of the sanction corresponds to the peculiarities of the specific case.

537. However, it is noted that the penalties provided for in items X, XI and XII only apply if the offender has already been sentenced to one of the sanctions of items II, III, IV, V and VI of the main section of Article 52, for the same specific case.

538. In Article 52, in its first paragraph, it is possible to understand the parameters established, as well as the objective criteria to be observed during the application of sanctions provided by the LGPD.

539. The criteria are the same as those observed in the legal culture of Brazil, of which:

(i) severity and nature of the infringement;
(ii) offender's good faith;
(iii) offender's economic condition;
(iv) recurrence, among others.

540. Within the parameters presented by the LGPD, two stand out for working as mechanisms for reducing penalties:

(a) The repeated and demonstrated adoption of internal mechanisms and procedures capable of minimizing damage and
(b) The adoption of good practices and governance policy.

541. Although the ANPD has not yet judged cases of noncompliance with the LGPD, there are already understandings in the Brazilian Court (Civil Court) that have adopted these mechanisms for reducing penalties, such as the reasoning presented by the judge who analyzed Public Civil Action 0020014 -30.2021.5.04.0261.

137. Brazil. Law 13.709 of Aug. 14, 2018, 2018.

542. In this case, the company brought to the records the information that it has a privacy manual, attached to page 183 et seq., in which there is, among others, designation of a person in charge, pursuant to Article 41 of the LGPD. Observing the hierarchical line drawn in the defense (not challenged by the Union), there is no evidence of a lack of functional autonomy necessary for the good performance of the position.

543. Furthermore, the Privacy Policy is outlined on page 194 and composes the internal rules for adapting the business structure to the legislation discussed in the specific case. Regarding security and prevention, the company also indicated the use of technological resources for data processing. The transparency portal indicated for the defense and the information brochures presented also show compliance with the principal criteria of free access and transparency.

544. The simple allegation that the company does not comply with the legal dictates deserves to be rejected in light of the evidence in the case file, as the company did not undertake to demonstrate compliance with the causes of request inferred as irregular by the Union.[138]

545. It is understood then that the national jurisprudence has guided its decisions on the weighting and balance of understandings involving the subject. Weighting is provided for in the content brought in the LGPD.

546. Therefore, it is noted that the objective of imposing administrative sanctions is to promote an institutional action focused on ensuring the security of information used by agents responsible for data processing.

547. And not in the mere accusation and imposition of drastic measures/penalties, as there is an understanding that the national authority must act in a balanced and educational manner.

548. This is added to the fact that ANPD is responsible and competent for the analysis of cases and the corresponding application of sanction measures and edition of guidelines for the performance of controlling entities, as indicated in Article 54:

> Art. 54. The value of the daily fine penalty applicable to violations of this Law must observe the seriousness of the offense and the extent of the damage or loss caused and be substantiated by the national authority.
>
> Single paragraph. The notice of the daily fine sanction must contain, at a minimum, the description of the obligation imposed, the reasonable period stipulated by the agency for its compliance and the amount of the daily fine to be applied for its noncompliance.[139]

138. Court of labor court of the 4th Region. Civil Public Civil Action 0020014-30.2021.5.04.0261. Jul. 13, 2021.
139. Brazil, Law 13.709 of Aug. 14, 2018, 2018.

549. This procedure must observe the limitations imposed by the constitutional principles of the country, with emphasis on the principle of proportionality and reasonableness.

550. It is also important to highlight that the national doctrine lists three interpretative parameters, which are:

- *Pertinence*: the adequacy, conformity or validity of the purpose achieved with the act—prohibition of discretion.
- *Necessity*: seeking not to exceed the indispensable limits for the conservation of the desired legitimate purpose.
- *Stricto sensu proportionality*: the result must contain the interests analyzed.

551. In other words, decisions must encompass these interpretive facets because the LGPD uses as a repressive mechanism the existence of penalties, which, in turn, affect companies of all sizes.

552. Due to this fact, the specific case must be analyzed with caution, as understood by Patrícia Peck:

> Observing the constitutional principle of proportionality, the attribution of sanctions must always observe proportionality as a criterion to prevent and inhibit possible abuses of state power when exercising their functions. Certainly, the new laws that deal with matters related to the protection of rights within the scope of the digital transformation of institutions have a very high impact on business models. Thus, one way to have them observed is to predict very high penalties. However, as these are rules that apply to any company profile, being a startup or a large multinational, private or public institution, from any sector of the economy, it is necessary to consider a dosage in the application of punishments, under penalty of making small business or even more innovative projects that tend to take more operational risks unfeasible.[140]

140. Patricia Peck Pinheiro, *Personal Data Protection: Comments on Law n. 13.709/2018* 157–158 (Editora SaraivaJur 3d ed. 2021).

Part IX. Specific Processing Situations

553. The Brazilian Data Protection Law (LGPD) does not have a chapter dedicated to specific processing situations as the European Union GDPR, i.e., Chapter 9. However, throughout the Brazilian law, legislators have included provisions addressing the topics that GDPR regulates specifically in its Articles 85 to 91.

554. Therefore, this part will focus on, from the LGPD standpoint: (i) processing for journalistic purposes and academic, artistic, or literary expression; (ii) processing of personal information versus public access to official documents; (iii) processing of the national identification number; (iv) processing in the context of employment; and (v) processing for scientific research, public archiving, and statistical purposes.

Chapter 1. Processing for Journalistic Purposes and Academic, Artistic or Literary Expression

555. According to the Brazilian Data Protection Law (LGPD), the processing of personal data for journalistic and artistic purposes or literary expression does not follow the rules established by the law, being one of the exemptions to the regulation that Article 4 sets out. This limitation to the scope of application of the law has the objective of reconciling the right to the protection of personal data with the right to freedom of expression and information.

556. The Constitution of the Federative Republic of Brazil regards freedom of expression as a fundamental right under Article 5. Therefore, the LGPD, by setting a derogation to the rules for processing personal data for journalistic and artistic purposes, provides legal certainty for journalists, book authors, and artists to perform their work without the fear of being punished when processing personal data.

557. However, it is important to bear in mind that freedom of expression is not an absolute right, which means that it can be limited or restricted in certain circumstances.

558. As a result, if a controller processing personal data for journalistic and artistic purposes violates the data subject's fundamental right to privacy, private life, honor, or image, the right to the freedom of expression will not be upheld (proportionality test applied to conflicting constitutional rights) and compensations for moral damages will be ensured.

559. The Brazilian judicial system has begun to issue decisions on the limits of personal data processing for journalistic purposes with the right to privacy, private life, honor, or image. In June 2021, the Court of Justice of the Federal District[141] upheld the decision made by the lower court, which found that a Brazilian newspaper had unlawfully processed personal data in a journalistic article, demanding that the media company compensate moral damages to the data subjects involved in the news story.

560. According to the Court, the newspaper, by publishing the plaintiffs' payrolls (which included personal data such as salary, name, and identification number), extrapolated the journalistic purposes and the right to inform. It is important to note that the lower court bore on a ruling from the Federal Supreme Court to apply the proportionality test between fundamental rights (privacy and freedom of expression and information). The media company has appealed the decision to the Superior Court of Justice, which has not yet issued an opinion on this case.

141. https://pje2i.tjdft.jus.br/consultapublica/ConsultaPublica/DetalheProcessoConsultaPublica/listView.seam?ca=fca930323cc01476b882b51518d471a45fd187ddfe216ebe.

561. As noted at the beginning of this chapter, the derogation provided for personal data processing for journalistic and artistic purposes has the goal of preventing journalism from censorship by agents of society who might claim breach of the right to privacy. However, journalists have been facing difficulties accessing information for journalistic matters due to controllers using LGPD to hold them.

562. Realizing this situation could become a standard practice by civil society and public authorities, the Brazilian Association of Investigative Journalism (ABRAJI) has published a written statement[142] expressing its disagreement with public and private organizations using LGPD to restrict the right to be informed, directing it to the ANPD, the Brazilian Councils of Justice (CNJ) and Public Prosecutor's Office (CNMP), and the Federal Court of Accounts (TCU).

563. Although the processing of personal data for journalistic and artistic purposes is an exemption to the LGPD, the above paragraphs have shown that specific requirements should be regarded when performing activities with private information from data subjects. It would be desired if the ANPD regulates this provision, bringing more legal certainty to the application of the data protection law.

564. Regarding the processing for academic purposes, even though it is also a derogation from specific Chapters of the law, the controller has yet to follow the requirements provided by Articles 7 (lawful basis for processing personal data) and 11 (lawful basis for processing sensitive personal data) when processing personal data for such scope.

565. The first question that arises when analyzing this provision refers to the definition of academic purposes since the LGPD does not classify it. Given the scope of the law, this expression should be regarded as processing personal data when performing academic productions, such as thesis, articles, and dissertations that may require the use of personal information from data subjects to state a scholarly opinion.

566. However, as established in Article 4, processing agents shall comply with the requirements for processing personal and sensitive data in accordance with Articles 7 and 11, respectively. Therefore, controllers and processors (acting on the former's behalf) should have a lawful basis provided by LGPD to process personal information from data subjects as well as meet certain conditions when performing any operation with sensitive personal data, such as applying anonymization techniques when possible.

142. https://www.abraji.org.br/noticias/abraji-e-mais-26-organizacoes-se-manifestam-contra-uso-indevido-da-lgpd.

567. Lastly, it is important to highlight that this enumerated instance shall not be applicable to educational sector companies when operating organizational activities. Such enterprises, i.e., schools, universities, and colleges, have to comply with the LGPD, especially when students process personal data for the admissions process and academic assessments.

568. The chart below provides an approximate comparison between the provisions of the LGPD and the GDPR regarding the processing for the purposes of this chapter:

LGPD	**GDPR**
Art. 7 This Law does not apply to the processing of personal data that: [...] II — is done exclusively: a) for journalistic and artistic purposes; or b) academic purposes, with Arts. 7 and 11 of this Law being applicable in these cases;	Article 85—Processing and freedom of expression and information 1. Member States shall by law reconcile the right to the protection of personal data pursuant to this Regulation with the right to freedom of expression and information, including processing for journalistic purposes and the purposes of academic, artistic or literary expression. 2. For processing carried out for journalistic purposes or the purpose of academic artistic or literary expression, Member States shall provide for exemptions or derogations from Chapter II (principles), Chapter III (rights of the data subject), Chapter IV (controller and processor), Chapter V (transfer of personal data to third countries or international organisations), Chapter VI (independent supervisory authorities), Chapter VII (cooperation and consistency) and Chapter IX (specific data processing situations) if they are necessary to reconcile the right to the protection of personal data with the freedom of expression and information.

LGPD	GDPR
	3. Each Member State shall notify to the Commission the provisions of its law which it has adopted pursuant to paragraph 2 and, without delay, any subsequent amendment law or amendment affecting them. Recital 153: Processing of Personal Data Solely for Journalistic Purposes or for the Purposes of Academic, Artistic or Literary Expression

Chapter 2. Processing of Personal Information Versus Public Access to Official Documents

569. The processing of personal information held in official documents, besides having to follow requirements provided by the LGPD (Part III of this monography), is subject to Federal Law No. 12.527/2011, known as the Access to Information Law, which regulates the freedom to access information guaranteed by the Constitution of the Federative Republic of Brazil in its Article 5, item XXXIII:

570. Article 5. All persons are equal before the law, without any distinction whatsoever, Brazilians and foreigners residing in the country being ensured of inviolability of the right to life, liberty, equality, security and property on the following terms:

> [...]
> XXXIII—all persons have the right to receive, from the public agencies, information of private interest to such persons, or of collective or general interest, which shall be provided within the period established by law, subject to liability, except for the information whose secrecy is essential to the security of society and of the State;

571. The Law is governed by the principles of transparency and publicity regarding the availability of information to public consultation by all persons. However, such principles are not absolute and do not apply to privileged or classified information held by public authorities. Article 3 of the Access to Information Law states that the legislation promotes the following guidelines:

- compliance with transparency as a general rule and secrecy as an exception;
- disclosure of information of public interest, regardless of requests;
- use of means of communication made possible by information technology;
- fostering the development of a culture of transparency in public administration;
- development of social control in public administration.

572. As stated in Articles 1 and 2, the Access to Information Law applies to all public bodies and private nonprofit enterprises. Thus, such private and public entities have to ensure all possible means to meet a natural person's request to access information held by them in accordance with Article 10. However, access to public information is not unlimited according to the above Law. According to Article 11, public authorities have the right not to make accessible public information classified or privileged.

573. In view of the presented situation, when one observes the clash of two fundamental principles (access to public information and protection of personal data), the most commonly adopted strategy is that of balancing through the use of the principle of proportionality.

574. By applying a judgment of proportionality, the goal is to establish, through observation of the current situation, the most viable way to ensure compatibility between the conflicting principles. That strategy seeks to ensure the maximum practical effectiveness of both principles while also establishing reciprocal limits between them so that the spirit of each of the principles is not silenced due to an alleged incompatibility.

575. In order to guide the better application of the proposed approach, in situations where we are faced with a dilemma involving access to public data and personal data protection, it is relevant to observe the extension of the damage to the subject within the current circumstance and to make a parallel with the public good that such action would provide for the society.[143]

576. When such strategy is applied, it turns clearly visible that the two legislations (LGPD and the Access to Information Law) harmonize and are systematically compatible with each other, reinforcing the guarantee of the fundamental rights and freedoms of citizens, at the same time that enforces transparency of public information and the processing of personal data for public purposes.

577. Contrary to the LGPD, the GDPR has a specific provision regulating public information processing. According to Article 86, the Regulation grants controllers, either public or private bodies, the right to disclose public information to perform a task carried out in the public interest. Additionally, as seen above in the Brazilian jurisdiction, the public authorities shall also observe requirements provided by the Union or Member State legislation to reconcile public access to official documents with the right to personal data protection.

578. The chart below provides an approximate comparison between the provisions of the LGPD and the GDPR regarding the processing for the purposes of this Chapter:

LGPD	GDPR
Art. 23 Processing of personal data by legal entities of public law referred to in sole paragraph of Art. 1 of Law No. 12,527, of November 18, 2011 (the "Brazilian Access to Information Law"), shall be done in fulfillment of its public purpose, in benefit of the public interest, for the	Article 86—Processing and public access to official documents Personal data in official documents held by a public authority or a public body or a private body for the performance of a task carried out in the public interest may be disclosed by the authority or body in accordance with Union or

143. Miguel Carbonell, *El Principio de Proporcionalidad y los Derechos Fundamentales*, in *El Principio de Proporcionalidad y la interpretación constitucional* 10 (Carbonell, Miguel ed., Ministerio de Justicia y Derechos Humanos 2008).

LGPD	GDPR
purpose of performing legal capabilities or discharging legal attributions of the public service, provided that: I — they communicate the situations in which, in the exercise of their regulatory capacities, they carry out the processing of personal data, supplying clear and up-to-date information about the legal base, purpose, procedures and practices used to carry out these activities in an easily accessible media, preferably on their websites; […] §3 The time periods and procedures for exercising data subjects' rights before the public authorities shall obey the provisions of specific legislation, especially the provisions stated in Law No. 9,507, of November 12, 1997 (the "Brazilian Habeas Data Law"), of Law No. 9,784, of January 29, 1999 (the "Federal Administrative Procedure Law"), and of Law No. 12,527, of November 18, 2011 (the "Brazilian Access to Information Law"). […] Art. 24 Public companies and mixed-capital companies that operate in the competing market, subject to the provisions of Art. 173 of the Federal Constitution, shall receive the same treatment given to private legal entities of private law, under the terms of this Law.	Member State law to which the public authority or body is subject in order to reconcile public access to official documents with the right to the protection of personal data pursuant to this Regulation. Recital 154: Principle of Public Access to Official Documents

LGPD	GDPR
Sole paragraph. Public and mixed-capital companies, when they are carrying out public policies and within the scope of their execution, shall receive the same treatment given to the bodies and entities of the public authorities, under the terms of this Chapter.	

579. As perceived, the Brazilian legislation does not directly address the discussed issue as does the GDPR. Although to portray LGPD's provisions and keep track of the best practices adopted internationally, the event called Civil Law Journey recently brought to discussion such case and had reached a conclusion.

580. The Civil Law Journey is an initiative of the Federal Court Council—CJF, and its main objective is to foster debate and propose statements on relevant and current themes of Brazilian private law, with the participation of the greatest national experts on the subjects discussed. During its ninth edition (2022), some statements about digital law were proposed, also reaching the topic of access to information and data protection. In this regard, the statement n. 688 was published:

> The Access to Information Law (LAI) and the General Law of Personal Data Protection (LGPD) establish compatible data management and protection systems. The LGPD does not exclude publicity and access to information in the terms of the LAI, based on the legal bases of Article 7, II or III, and Article 11, II, a or b, of the General Law of Data Protection.[144]

581. In conclusion, as noted above, besides the absence of a normative provision concerning the relation between access to information and data protection, the Brazilian legal community had already recognized the compatibility of the two legislation and should, in a timely fashion, apply such understanding in case law and norms.

144. Centro de Estudos Judiciários. *IX Jornada Direito Civil: comemoração dos 20 anos da Lei n. 10.406/2022 e da instituição da Jornada de Direito Civil: enunciados aprovados* 48 (Conselho da Justiça Federal, Centro de Estudos Judiciários 2022).

Chapter 3. Processing of the National Identification Number

582. The processing of the national identification number has not been addressed explicitly by LGPD, as GDPR does with its Article 87. The GDPR has entrusted the EU Member States the authority to specify other conditions for processing a national identification number than the ones already established by the Regulation.

583. In accordance with the LGPD, a national identification number is considered personal data, as, with this information, it is possible to identify a natural person. Because of that, the processing of this personal data shall comply with the requirements provided by Article 7 as well as with the principles of Article 6, especially purpose, necessity, and transparency.

584. In this regard, when controllers, either public or private organizations that observe the general provisions of the law, collect such personal data, they shall state a specific purpose for carrying out this processing activity, among transparency details, for instance, the duration of the operation and the data subjects' rights (Article 18, LGPD—Part IV of this monograph).

585. The Brazilian Federal Government has enacted Law no 14.129/2021, regulating the principles, rules, and instruments to implement e-government mechanisms. The sole paragraph of Article 1 of the Law expressly states that the federal public bodies subject to the rules shall comply with the LGPD when deploying technological resources for bureaucratic and administrative activities.

586. Regarding the national identification number (CPF), the Law sets out that this personal data shall be primarily the information to identify a Brazilian citizen. For this reason, the above Law requires that the documents listed in paragraph one of Article 28 of this Law shall contain the CPF as well as the public bodies' databases. This requirement follows the rule established by Article 25 of the LGPD, which sets out that the data shall be structured in standard data formats and communication protocols, hence, data interoperability.

587. Besides complying with technical and organizational information security measures, the controllers shall elect a lawful basis for processing data subjects' national identification numbers for a specific purpose. As seen in Part III of this monograph, Article 7 of the LGPD presents the legal grounds for carrying out operations with personal information.

588. Thus, it might be the case that organizations need to collect data subjects' national identification numbers for compliance with a legal or regulatory obligation imposed for them, for instance, the issuance of invoice (Federal Law No. 8.846/1994). The processing of this personal data might also occur when controllers sign contracts with data subjects, as the party's qualification part of the agreement has its national identification number.

589. However, retail companies' standard practice is to ask data subjects to provide such personal data for access benefits. Because of this, in 2021, the National Secretariat of Consumers (SENACOM), a public body linked to the Ministry of Justice and Public Security, launched a preliminary investigation to assess whether pharmacies are violating data protection rules by requesting consumers to hand in their national identification number in order to receive purchase discounts.[145]

590. Therefore, although the ANPD has not yet issued guidance on how to process data subjects' national identification numbers lawfully, and there has not yet been any formal conclusion from investigative authorities (ANPD and SENACOM) regarding abuse of this personal data, controllers must follow the requirements laid down by the LGPD to be in compliance with all the activities regarding operations with citizens' CPF.

591. The chart below provides an approximate comparison between the provisions of the LGPD and the GDPR regarding the processing for the purposes of this chapter:

LGPD	GDPR
Art. 7 Processing of personal data shall only be carried out under the following circumstances: [...]	Article 87—Processing of the national identification number Member States may further determine the specific conditions for the processing of a national identification number or any other identifier of general application. In that case the national identification number or any other identifier of general application shall be used only under appropriate safeguards for the rights and freedoms of the data subject pursuant to this Regulation.

145. https://www.defesadoconsumidor.gov.br/portal/ultimas-noticias/2015-redes-de-drogarias-sao-notificadas-pelo-ministerio-da-justica-e-seguranca-publica-por-possivel-infracao-a-lei-de-protecao-de-dados.

Chapter 4. Processing in the Context of Employment

592. The LGPD does not directly address the processing in the context of employment. The Brazilian law only generically relates the possibilities that enable the processing of personal data, presenting some legal grounds that are commonly also adopted in labor circumstances.

593. As will be observed in the chart below, the LGPD mentions the possibility of processing the subject's personal data in order to comply with legal regulations and when the data is necessary for the execution of a contract. These two legal grounds for the processing are commonly seen as justification for the processing in the context of employment since the employee data is necessary for the controller to positively respond to official regulatory demands and also to promote the hiring and working of the employees for the controller.

594. In contrast, the GDPR objectively addresses the related theme, presenting provisions specifically created to legislate the processing of personal data in the context of employment, seeking to preserve the fundamental rights of the employees, creating limits for the controller's power over the processing and reinforcing the subject's rights. The chart below provides an approximate comparison between the provisions of the LGPD and the GDPR regarding the processing for the purposes of this chapter:

LGPD	GDPR
Art. 7 Processing of personal data shall only be carried out under the following circumstances: II — for the controller's compliance with legal or regulatory obligations; […] V — when necessary for the execution of a contract or preliminary procedures related to a contract to which the data subject is a party, at the data subject's request; […]	Article 88—Processing in the context of employment 1. Member States may, by law or by collective agreements, provide for more specific rules to ensure the protection of the rights and freedoms in respect of the processing of employees' personal data in the employment context, in particular for the purposes of the recruitment, the performance of the contract of employment, including discharge of obligations laid down by law or by collective agreements, management, planning and organization of work, equality and diversity in the workplace, health and safety at work, protection of employer's or customer's property and for the purposes of the exercise and enjoyment, on an individual or collective basis, of rights and benefits related to

LGPD	GDPR
Article 11 The processing of sensitive personal data shall only occur in the following situations: II — without providing the owner's consent, in the hypotheses in which it is indispensable for: a) compliance with legal or regulatory obligations by the controller; [...]	employment, and for the purpose of the termination of the employment relationship. 2. Those rules shall include suitable and specific measures to safeguard the data subject's human dignity, legitimate interests and fundamental rights, with particular regard to the transparency of processing, the transfer of personal data within a group of undertakings, or a group of enterprises engaged in a joint economic activity and monitoring systems at the work place. 3. Each Member State shall notify to the Commission those provisions of its law which it adopts pursuant to paragraph 1, by 25 May 2018 and, without delay, any subsequent amendment affecting them. Recital 155: Processing in the Employment Context

§1. The Brazilian Data Protection Law in Labor and Human Resources

595. The Brazilian Data Protection Law emerged from the social and techno logical evolution that made it essential to regulate issues and situations related to privacy and protection of personal data, whether in physical or digital media. Personal data processing activities carried out by individuals or legal entities, private or public, are now obliged to respect and comply with the rules of this specific law.

596. As a result, the application of it takes place in all sectors of the economy and in all branches of law and may be complementary or subsidiary whenever there is some type of activity for the processing of personal data, as occurs, for example, in working relationships.

597. As in many countries around the world, data protection is primarily intended to protect fundamental freedoms and rights, bring legal security and guidance to data subjects and processing agents, as well as establish uniform rules and criteria for a lived reality by the information society.

598. When we talk about this law and labor, we must think about an environment where the activities of processing personal data are constant and, with even greater potential, in certain sectors, such as HR.

599. Citizens spend a lot of their life in the workplace. The worker's daily routine involves the execution of tasks that may culminate in the processing of personal data and, therefore, the knowledge of the Brazilian Data Protection Law in labor relations becomes mandatory, both in the sense of seeing the worker and employer as data holders and personal data processing agents.

600. The Brazilian data protection law aims to establish the bases, principles and procedures to guarantee the right of all people to the lawful processing of their personal data, its protection, as well as the exercise of their rights.

601. Regarding labor relations, we must apply Brazil's data protection law in various situations and in the HR department's work routine. We have the so-called pre-contractual phases, the validity of the employment contract and the post-contractual phase or after the termination of the employment relationship.

602. The pre-contractual phase is the phase of the potential employee's first contact with the future employer. As previously observed, for this phase, the LGPD authorizes the processing of personal data whenever such activity is necessary for the execution of the preliminary procedures related to the labor contract (Article 7º, V, LGPD).

603. The preliminary phase is well-known by most of the population. Anyone has probably already turned in their résumé somewhere to apply for a job or participated in a job selection interview. It is important to highlight that nowadays, this pre-contractual phase can be carried out by third parties (recruiting company, recruitment website, etc.), which is a common procedure in many institutions.

604. As one of the fundamental principles of the Brazilian data protection law is nondiscrimination (Article 6º, IX, LGPD), during the pre-contractual phase, it is important to pay attention to the methods used, which cannot generate any discriminatory criteria between candidates. From this premise, we enter the area of sensitive data collection, such as, for example, requesting pregnancy or drug tests, which will contain the candidate's health data, in addition to having high discriminatory potential. Unfortunately, such methods were used a lot by recruiters and with that, they harmed many candidates.

605. It should be noted that there are exceptions provided by law for requesting the aforementioned exams and that, in the light of the regulation, they would not constitute a discriminatory processing of personal data but rather a treatment supported by a legal basis of compliance with a legal obligation, as in case of a request for a drug test for a candidate for professional driver[146] or for a psychotechnical test and a certificate of criminal background for the candidate to exercise the duty of security guard.[147]

606. As an innovation brought by the data protection law and which sheds light on the part of the recruitment and selection procedure for workers, organizations are now obliged to clearly inform unselected candidates what form of treatment the personal data provided will have within that institution until reaching the end of the data life cycle by eliminating all databases or anonymizing them. This transparency mechanism, in addition to fulfilling the objectives of the law (Article 6º, VI, LGPD), is essential to guarantee the rightfulness of the data processing and the due respect for the subject's rights.

607. In the contractual phase, that is, during the term of the employment contract, the worker will have contact with the organization's internal policies and regulations, including provisions involving privacy and data protection.

608. At this stage, we have a great imbroglio between employee and employer. The fact that the labor legislation establishes subordination as one of the requirements for the concept of employment relationship is seen by many scholars as a way of imposing worker acceptance on any and all data processing modalities.

609. Labor relations are private relations established between the employer and the employee in which there is, as a rule, an economic and social inequality that makes the power of the parties asymmetric, especially due to the employee's vulnerability and low sufficiency.

---

146. Article 168 of the Brazilian Labour Law: A medical examination will be mandatory, on behalf of the employer, under the conditions established in this article and in the additional instructions to be issued by the Ministry of Labor:

    § 6. Toxicological tests will be required, prior to admission and at the time of dismissal, in the case of a professional driver, guaranteed the right to a counter-test in case of positive result and the confidentiality of the results of the respective exams.

147. Law No. 7102/1983: Art. 12—The directors and other employees of specialized companies cannot have a registered criminal record.
    Law No. 7102/1983: Art. 16—For the exercise of the profession, the guard will meet the following requirements:

    — have passed a physical, mental and psychotechnical health exam;
    — not having a registered criminal record; and

    Law no. 10.826/2003: Art. 4 In order to acquire a firearm for permitted use, the interested party must, in addition to declaring the effective need, meet the following requirements:

    — Proof of suitability, with the presentation of clearance certificates from criminal records provided by the Federal, State, Military and Electoral Courts and of not responding to a police inquiry or criminal process, which may be provided by electronic means.

610. The fact is that not all treatment activities and personal data may be carried out without the specific consent of the worker. There will be those arising from a legal obligation that must be complied with by the employer regardless of the express demonstration of the worker, the holder. However, there will be activities that will depend on the employee's consent so that they are valid and can be carried out, such as the collection and exhibition of photographs that identify the worker and do not have informational and institutional purposes. Using the employee's image for an external marketing campaign, for example, will depend on the employee's consent in a free, unambiguous and informed manner.

611. The main discussion that arises from this situation is related to the necessity that the employee's consent shall be freely given. In a labor relation, it is common to see the subordination of the employee, who might follow all the determinations of the employer in order to keep its place in the company. In such scenario, it is hard to guarantee that the employee's consent to any processing led by the data controller is freely given, which represents a huge lack of legality in such processing.

612. In such circumstances, it is essential that the data controller ensures the freedom for the employee to consent or not with the processing, following every normative provision presented in Article 8° of LGPD and making the processing activity valid and legit.

613. Eventually, the worker may leave his/her job or may be dismissed at the employer's discretion. At this stage, compliance with the data protection law principles is also mandatory since the Law itself expressly states the duty to provide information on the completion of personal data processing activities and, furthermore, that there is transparency in the entire procedure, and the law itself may holder of the right to request this information from the employer.

614. When we talk about labor relations, there are several legal obligations to be fulfilled, including the custody of physical or digital documents, and the storage of these documents also characterizes an activity of processing personal data. In order to fulfill those obligations, the processing activity shall be carried on with bases on Article 7°, II, LGPD, which authorizes the data processing for compliance with a legal or regulatory obligation by the controller.

615. The duty of custody of documents must respect a reasonable period of storage, being illicit to guard for a period longer than necessary or stipulated by law, depending on the situation.

616. This is also an important point that involves data protection law and labor. The so-called document temporality table is a good help in organizing institutions to prepare themselves to adapt to the law and to train their employees to respect its adequacy.

§2. AUTOMATED DECISION IN RECRUITMENT AND SELECTION PROCESSES

617. With the recurrent use of new technologies, especially Artificial Intelligence, many organizations use automated procedures for the selection of personnel. Here we are faced with a recurrent question: what are the risks to the fundamental rights of workers when selection processes are guided by automated decisions?

618. Attention should be paid to the fact that the construction of corporate governance that respects the dictates of personal data regulation cannot contribute to any discriminatory practice which can occur in automated processes.

619. We can find some information and communication technology (ICT) in the processes of hiring workers to assess their performance and provide professional advancement in the form of promotion, control of the work routine, mobility and displacement to the workplace, among others. The dilemma begins when analyzing that the behavior of technology can adopt might be discriminatory, exclusionary and invasive measures since the automated process that depends on algorithms and machine learning can trigger episodes of bias.

620. A single job opening can be sought after by a large number of applicants. Thus, the organization uses algorithmic technology to filter candidate profiles from the start, often with the justification of seeking to optimize the process by analyzing the information entered by data subjects in their resumes.

621. Initially, the candidate's selection occurs according to criteria established by machines and not by human judgment, and the algorithms have limited decision-making capacity and are based on criteria acquired in learning, with the feeding of a database and mathematical formulas that, despite being an exact science, they can result in inaccurate information, with an incomplete description or even untrue.

622. A study by Mathematics Cathy O'Neil[148] demonstrates how technology and artificial intelligence, when used in job applicants' selection processes, can distort reality and generate decisions with discriminatory, segregated and unfair criteria.

623. In the book *Weapons of Math Destruction: How Big Data Increases Inequality and Threatens Democracy*, which refers to an anecdote with the expression "weapons of mass destruction," O'Neil analyzes, at a socioeconomic level, the dangers of automating processes by algorithms and big data analysis systems, based on examples from the US, in order to reflect how these technological tools can reproduce the prejudices of their formulators, linking inequality dynamics.[149]

148. Cathy O'Neil earned a Ph.D. in Math from Harvard, was a postdoc at the MIT math department, and a professor at Barnard College where she published a number of research papers in arithmetic algebraic geometry. https://hdsr.mitpress.mit.edu/pub/j8y5fwco/release/1. Access on Nov. 17, 2021.

149. Cathy O'Neil, *Weapons of Math Destruction: How Big Data Increases Inequality and Threatens Democracy* (Crown Publishing Group (NY) 2016). Available at: https://edisciplinas.usp.br/plugin

624. In the economic realm, most organizations are looking for ways to control the productivity of the workforce, increase profits, facilitate the inflow of capital and decrease maintenance expenses. With that, many develop the thought that using technology is the way that will best provide the desired objective without, however, observing the ethical issues that may arise.

625. The improvement of corporate management, in times of development of digital rights, must always pay attention to the minimum necessary and at least invasive, which also fits into the routine of recruitment and selection procedures for workers.

626. The way in which technology is used to gather information about workers applying for a job vacancy and the justification for promoting a selection based on data, given the impact that this technology can have on the employment relationship, refers us to Article 20 of the General Law of Protection of Personal Data.

627. Article 20[150] deals with the data subject's right to challenge the automated decision. It is important to highlight that there is no legal provision of the impediment to being submitted to an automated decision but a right to review any fully automated decision that affects, in any sense, the interest of the holder of personal data or causes him any harm.

628. Therefore, we can say that the decisions include, but are not limited to, those related to the formation of behavioral profiles, and, of course, there is no obligation to verify a violation of specific rights for which Article 20 of the Brazilian data protection law can be invoked by the holder, as long as the fully automated decision affects any interest of the holder.

§3. Internal Adjustments to Meet the Rights of Employees in Relation to the Brazilian Data Protection Law

629. As a data holder, the worker may, at any time, exercise the rights provided for in the LGPD. This implies saying that the organization must have mechanisms to meet the rights of all holders, not just workers.

---

file.php/5971949/mod_resource/content/1/%28FFLCH%29%20BOOK%20Weapons%20of%20Math%20Destruction%20-%20Cathy %20ONeal.pdf. Access on Nov. 17, 2021.

150. Law 13.709/18. Art. 20. The data subject has the right to request a review of decisions taken solely on the basis of automated processing of personal data that affect their interests, including decisions designed to define their personal, professional, consumer and credit profile or the aspects of your personality.

§ 1 The controller shall provide, whenever requested, clear and adequate information regarding the criteria and procedures used for the automated decision, observing commercial and industrial secrets.

§ 2 In case the information referred to in § 1 of this article is not offered, based on the observance of commercial and industrial secrets, the national authority may carry out an audit to verify discriminatory aspects in the automated processing of personal data.

630. Compliance with the Brazilian data protection law involves several internal procedures and depends on the collaboration of all involved parties. Starting with the link between the organization, the owner and ANPD, the person in charge of personal data.

631. This figure is extremely important in structuring the corporate environment to meet the rights of holders and to raise awareness of data protection in an institutional way.

632. Data protection and best practices in the work environment deal directly with the impact of the law on the employment relationship and also with other laws that deal with privacy and data protection, even if sparsely.

633. The DPO becomes crucial in meeting the requests of the holders and must have their identity published so that the holder knows to whom they must report to send their inquiries and requests. Furthermore, the organization must have a service channel that can be accessed easily by the owner, according to the previously observed Article 41 of LGPD.

634. Workers, like any other individuals holding personal data, have the right to gain access to the information that is held about them. This right applies, for example, to records that the employer has on worker illnesses (occupational or not), disciplinary or training records, access controls and emails, paper or scanned documents, and audit trails, among others.

635. Training on data protection can expand the understanding of employees on the subject, which will help in the organization's Compliance.

§4. Preparation of the Employee to Avoid Violations of Personal Data

636. The legislation also has an informational and educational character. The subject of "privacy and data protection" is relatively new and still not widespread in some sectors.

637. Therefore, those responsible for processing activities must collaborate with law enforcement to permanently train and update all their servers in matters of personal data protection, which can be done through the delivery of courses, seminars, workshops and any other form of teaching in person or even virtualized.

638. All aspects of the Brazilian data protection law are relevant to all organizations, regardless of the size, economic power and nature of their business. Compliance with this law also involves the informational and educational nature of the law.

639. Within the labor relations scenario, which has specific contours, the existence of good practices, training, internal rules and continuous improvement of processing activities becomes a means of minimizing or even mitigating the internal risks that can generate a personal data breach. For this matter, Article 50 of LGPD emphasizes the importance for every processing agent to have its own data governance structure and to constantly review and update it, creating means to pass to the employees how to comply with the law and internal regulations during the execution of the day-a-day activities.

640. The worker must be taught not only to carry out personal data processing operations but to carry them out in accordance with the law, to meet the need for the purposes of his work.

641. Imagine how the organization's performance will improve once the worker understands that it is not allowed to communicate personal data with third parties unless there is a justification, a legal basis. Teach that employees cannot make copies on their own, on USB devices or other types of devices, of personal data that the organization has in its database. Upload a nonworking file to the corporate cloud, then.

642. These are common situations that can trigger personal data breaches. Therefore, it is essential that institutions, within their competence, promote programs and study plans, books and materials with content on the right to the protection of personal data, as well as a culture of exercise and institutional respect for the rights of the holders.

Chapter 5. Processing for Scientific Research, Public Archiving, and Statistical Purposes

643. According to the LGPD, controllers who qualify as a research entity (Article 5, IX, LGPD: body or entity of the direct or indirect public administration or private nonprofit legal entity legally constituted under Brazilian laws, with headquarters and jurisdiction in the country, which includes in its institutional mission or social or statutory objective basic or applied research of a historical, scientific, technological or statistical nature) are allowed to process personal and sensitive data for carrying out studies, in accordance with Articles 7 and 11, respectively. However, when performing activities with personal information for this purpose, controllers shall ensure, whenever possible, the anonymization of personal data.

644. Article 13 of the LGPD provides specific rules for carrying out public health studies. When accessing and extracting personal data databases for this purpose, research entities shall keep them in a controlled and secure environment, ensuring the application of anonymization or pseudonymization techniques of the data. When releasing the results of clinical trials, the research entities shall under no circumstances reveal personal data.

645. The GDPR has similar provisions regulating the processing for scientific purposes, as prescribed in Article 89. The Regulation states that the operation activity carried out by controllers shall be subject to appropriate safeguards (i.e., pseudonymization or anonymization) designed to ensure respect for the principles of data minimization, proportionality, and necessity, as the rights and freedoms of the data subject.

646. It is important to establish a parallel between the GDPR and LGPD provisions. In European law, any data processor can perform the processing of personal and sensitive data for carrying out studies, not only the research entities. By contrast, according to Brazilian legislation, only research entities are truly eligible to process personal data for research activities.

647. Concerning the interpretation of Article 89 of the GDPR, it is important to highlight the Recitals, which clarify the meaning of the rules for processing agents and authorities.

648. Recital No. 156 reminds controllers that the processing of personal data for scientific purposes should also comply with relevant legislation, such as on clinical trials. An example is provided by Recital No. 161, which states that, according to Regulation No. 536/2014 of the European Parliament of the EU, controllers shall obtain the data subjects' consent in compliance with the requirements of Regulation 536.

649. In the Brazilian jurisdiction, the application of other relevant legislation regarding the processing for scientific purposes shall also be borne in mind by controllers. For instance, procedures for clinical trials are well regulated by administrative statutes passed by public bodies, especially the Brazilian National Council of Health (CNS).

650. Therefore, when processing for clinical trials, controllers shall also observe Resolution No. 466/2021[151] of the CNS, which provides guidance for research entities and researchers to develop clinical trials in accordance with the Law. One of the requirements that CNS demands is the need to obtain an Informed Consent Agreement, in which it shall be clarified for the participants (data subjects) the nature of the research, its objectives, methods, expected benefits, potential risks, and safeguard measures implemented to guarantee the participants' confidentiality and privacy.

651. Regarding the processing for public archiving, the LGPD has not addressed it specifically in any provision. However, controllers shall follow the requirements for performing activities with personal data for this purpose, such as having a lawful legal basis as well as providing transparency details about the processing of the data subject.

652. It is important to highlight that, regarding the processing for public archiving, Federal Law No. 12.527/2011, known as the Access to Information Law, guarantees to every citizen (hence, data subjects) in its Article 7 the right to obtain information registered by public bodies or private nonprofit entities in public archives.

653. When processing personal data for public archiving purposes, controllers have to be aware of three factors,[152] which are: (1) balancing the data subject right to privacy with the public interest aim of the public archives for society; (2) ensuring information security techniques when storing the documents, preserving their authenticity, reliability and accuracy; and (3) providing safeguards for protecting data subjects' right to privacy and data protection when processing personal data in technological means.

654. In pursuance of compliance with the LGPD rules, public archives shall observe the implementation of certain actions, such as: (1) providing a privacy notice for the data subject and establishing a data protection policy with regard to the purpose of the processing; (2) performing DPIAs to mitigate possible risks arising from the processing of sensitive personal data or large amounts of data; (3) publishing Terms of Access to the public archive, designing rules in accordance with the Access to Information Law and the LGPD for accessing documents archived either physically or digitally.

---

151. https://conselho.saude.gov.br/resolucoes/2012/466_english.pdf.
152. https://periodicos.ufpb.br/index.php/archeion/article/view/57020.

655. However, Article 89 of the GDPR expressly states that this purpose should be performed in the public interest. Recital 158 provides clear guidance concerning the interpretation of processing for public archiving, such as that the public authorities or public or private bodies that hold data of public interest should be services that have a legal obligation to process (acquire, preserve, appraise, arrange, describe, communicate, promote, disseminate and provide access to such personal data).

656. Moreover, because records of public interest might include data from deceased persons, the above Recital also sets forth that the GDPR does not apply to this situation, as it will not be considered personal data under the Regulation. Lastly, EU Member States are authorized to process personal data for arching purposes when providing specific information related to historical facts that occurred in the past regarding political behavior under former totalitarian state regimes, genocide, crimes against humanity, or war crimes.

657. As for the processing for statistical purposes, the LGPD does not provide specific rules concerning this activity with personal data. The only moment the Brazilian Law refers to the term "statistic" is when it presents the meaning of research entities in Article 5. However, with the objective of understanding how the process of personal data for statistical purposes should happen in accordance with the Law, we shall examine how the GDPR addresses it.

658. As seen with the processing for scientific purposes, Article 89 of the GDPR also regulates how personal data are processed for statistical purposes. Paragraph 1 of this article states that controllers shall implement safeguards (technical and organizational measures such as pseudonymization or anonymization) to ensure respect for the principles of data minimization, proportionality, and necessity. Paragraph 2 also assures the EU and the Member States to establish derogations from the data subjects' rights of Articles 15, 16, 18 and 21 (Part IV of this monography) if the safeguards are ensured by the controllers.

659. Additionally, Recital 162 provides further guidance for processing agents. This statement defines what the Regulation considers as "statistical purposes," being any operation of collection and the processing of personal data necessary for statistical surveys or the production of statistical results. The Recital recognizes that the result of statistical purposes is not personal data but aggregate data, which are used in support of measures or decisions regarding nonidentifiable natural persons.

660. Therefore, concerning the application of the LGPD for processing personal data for statistical purposes, controllers shall ensure that technical and organizational measures are in place in order to protect data subjects' right to privacy as well as electing a lawful basis for carrying out the processing, according to Articles 6, 7 and 9 of the LGPD. This operation activity frequently happens with organizations using strategy techniques of business intelligence (BI) to help them make decisions more accurately and have a better analytical examination of data sets produced by the businesses.

661. In conclusion, when processing personal data for the purpose of producing statistical reports, controllers should apply some measures, such as: (1) structuring a new database with data anonymized or pseudonymized collected from the user database in order to prevent identifying directly or indirectly a natural person; and (2) applying safe techniques of database disposal, when the purpose for the processing is no longer necessary.

662. The chart below provides an approximate comparison between the provisions of the LGPD and the GDPR regarding the processing for the purposes of this chapter:

LGPD	GDPR
Art. 4 This Law does not apply to the processing of personal data that: […] II — is done exclusively: a) for journalistic and artistic purposes; or	Article 89—Safeguards and derogations relating to processing for archiving purposes in the public interest, scientific or historical research purposes or statistical purposes 1. Processing for archiving purposes in the public interest, scientific or historical research purposes or statistical purposes, shall be subject to appropriate safeguards, in accordance with this Regulation, for the rights and freedoms of the data subject. 2 Those safeguards shall ensure that technical and organisational measures are in place in particular in order to ensure respect for the principle of data minimisation. 3 Those measures may include pseudonymisation provided that those purposes can be fulfilled in that manner. 4 Where those purposes can be fulfilled by further processing which does not permit or no longer permits the identification of data subjects, those purposes shall be fulfilled in that manner. 2. Where personal data are processed for scientific or historical research purposes or statistical purposes, Union or Member State law may provide for derogations from the rights referred to in Articles 15, 16, 18 and 21 subject to the conditions and safeguards referred to in paragraph 1 of this Article in so far as such rights are likely to render impossible or seriously impair the achievement of the specific purposes, and such derogations are necessary for the fulfilment of those purposes.

LGPD	GDPR
	3. Where personal data are processed for archiving purposes in the public interest, Union or Member State law may provide for derogations from the rights referred to in Articles 15, 16, 18, 19, 20 and 21 subject to the conditions and safeguards referred to in paragraph 1 of this Article in so far as such rights are likely to render impossible or seriously impair the achievement of the specific purposes, and such derogations are necessary for the fulfilment of those purposes. 4. Where processing referred to in paragraphs 2 and 3 serves at the same time another purpose, the derogations shall apply only to processing for the purposes referred to in those paragraphs. Recital 156: Processing for Archiving, Scientific or Historical Research or Statistical Purposes. Recital 157: Information from Registries and Scientific Research. Recital 158: Processing for Archiving Purposes. Recital 159: Processing for Scientific Research Purposes Recital 160: Processing for Historical Research Purposes Recital 161: Consenting to the Participation in Clinical Trials. Recital 162: Processing for Statistical Purposes Recital 163: Production of European and National Statistics

Part X. Specific Data Protection Regimes

663. There is huge complexity in taking care of personal and sensitive data that requires specific and demanding confidentiality measures in order to guarantee the security of the subject's information. Most of the time, it happens to professional secrecy, especially when it is related to medical care and secrecy of legal relations, which possess a Code of Ethics to ordinate the professionals' actions, which violations may imply in crimes identified by the Brazilian Criminal Code. It can also relate to matters that are concerned about the activities of churches and religious associations, but the national authority still has not addressed such topics.

664. There are specific provisions in the LGPD that calls for a specialized and differentiated regime of information security and data protection, seeking to assure the subject's informational self-determination. This kind of treatment can be observed in topics related to client-lawyer confidentiality and also for health data, for example. It is important to highlight that the legislation also brought greater protection for personal data classified as sensitive, such as health data. Thus, if there is any data breach, or even undue sharing, without authorization of the holder, high penalties may be imposed on the controller (person who collects the personal data), in addition, of course, to damage to the data subjects.

665. Thus, it can be affirmed that the LGPD was conceived with the purpose of bringing more clarity and responsibility in the use of the data of individuals, also bringing a penalty for those who do not comply with the rules established in the Law regarding the collection, storage, processing and sharing of personal data.

Chapter 1. Obligations of Professional Secrecy

666. The data protection law carries in its scope that health professionals and organizations are required to keep their patients' information confidential. Thus, as already widely addressed in this article, personal data are the owner of the holder, and their nature is private; that is, if any processing is required on top of that data, it is necessary to obtain his consent.

667. When we talk about the activity of law, there is already a protection brought by the Federal Constitution. As provided in Article 133,[153] "the lawyer is indispensable to the administration of justice, being inviolable for his acts and manifestations in the exercise of the profession, within the limits of the law."

668. Together with the Magna Carta, it can also be brought that the professional practice of law is regulated by Law 8.906/1994, the Statute of the Brazilian Law Firm and Bar Association.

669. However, there is no doubt that law firms and lawyers are subject to Law No. 13,709/2018—General Data Protection Law (LGPD). Law firms are legal entities under private law, and lawyers are natural persons framed by the Law as responsible for their compliance.

670. The autonomy of the profession and professional secrecy are not at risk either with the application of the Law or with the supervisory action of the ANPD. They are even reinforced by it.

671. The data are protected by professional secrecy, both in relation to the ANPD, which may not have access to them, and when captured for professional purposes of the law, as they are protected against their leakage or undue treatment. In this case, it includes disclosure or use for purposes other than those for which they were captured.

672. In Article 6, I of the LGPD, we have the following: "Art. 6º The activities of processing personal data must observe the good faith and the following principles: I—purpose: carrying out the processing for legitimate, specific, explicit and informed purposes to the holder, without the possibility of further processing in a manner incompatible with these purposes."

673. It will be up to the OAB, through its Ethics and Discipline Courts, in addition to conducting the judgment of the issue, to decide, depending on the situation, whether to send a letter to the ANPD or not for action. In parallel, the ANPD may act independently of the OAB.

---

153. Constitution of the Federative Republic of Brazil, Art. 133.

674. Therefore, the OAB and the ANPD will act together in compliance with data protection rules, always respecting the prerogatives of lawyers and the protection given to the profession by the Federal Constitution. Just a quick reminder, the rules are not only entered in the LGPD, but they are also inserted in the Civil Code, Consumer Protection Code, and other Brazilian's laws.

675. It is important that lawyers and law firms, in a posture of institutional union, maintain absolute rightness in the processing of data in order not to expose the profession, as a whole, to the risk of concussion in the confidence of their image: data leakage or irregular treatment could cause a public exposure of the profession, and it could bring difficult-to-reverse damage.

676. The exceptions for the application of the LGPD to lawyers and law firms are only those provided for by the law itself, among them, anonymization of data, processing for the purposes of public security, criminal prosecution, for exclusively journalistic, artistic or academic purposes.

Chapter 2. Law Enforcement Agencies

677. ANPD is the public agency responsible for enforcing the data protection law. However, it is not clear if other government agencies are also entitled. Some agencies are working coordinately to enforce the data protection law.

678. The LGPD (Brazilian Data Protection Law) establishes that ANPD (Brazilian Data Protection Agency) is responsible for ensuring data protection in Brazil, as well as supervising and applying sanctions when personal data is processed without compliance with what is established by law. Furthermore, the LGPD determines that ANPD shall liaise with public regulatory authorities to exercise their powers in specific sectors of economic and governmental activities subject to regulation.

679. ANPD, initially, was not an independent agency, functioning under the Institutional Security Cabinet of the Presidency, which means that resources to maintain the agency came from this administrative body. Notwithstanding, the recently approved Law n. 14.460/2022 has transformed ANPD into an autarchy, which gives the authority complete financial and functional autonomy, following the best practices already taken in other countries.

680. Decree 10,474/2020 structured ANPD. It is constituted by a board of directors, the highest management body, and a National Council of Data Privacy and Protection, which propose strategic guidelines and provide subsidies to the elaboration of the National Data Privacy and Protection Policy and for ANDP performance.

681. Besides the work from ANPD, as mentioned in Part 1, one main piece of legislation applied in data protection situations is the Consumer Defense Code. The regulatory agencies responsible for enforcing the consumer law are the state consumer agencies and the state prosecutors.

682. It is very clear in which ways ANPD shall act to ensure data protection in Brazil. However, it is not clear what the limits are from other government regulatory authorities, such as the consumer ones. Therefore, consumers, state regulatory agencies, and state prosecutors are taking action to enforce LGPD.

683. The state prosecutors belong to the Public Attorney's Office, and they can act to protect natural and collective rights.

> Article 129. The following are institutional functions of the Public Prosecution: (CA No. 45, 2004)
>
> I — to initiate, exclusively, public criminal prosecution, under the terms of the law;
> II — to ensure effective respect by the Public Authorities and by the services of public relevance for the rights guaranteed in this Constitution, taking the action required to guarantee such rights;

III — to institute civil investigation and public civil suit to protect public and social property, the environment and other diffuse and collective interests (…)

684. Hence, some of them understood they were entitled to data protection enforcement. Likewise, the consumer state regulatory agencies, understanding data subjects as consumers, also have started to take measures to enforce LGPD.

685. This is not positive since it can cause a double charge considering the same fact, and that is why it is being questioned.

686. Despite that fact, there are some public regulatory agencies that are working coordinately to enforce data protection. At the beginning of May 2021, the Administrative Council for Consumer Defense (Cade), responsible for analyzing mergers and acquisitions, the General Public Attorney's Office (MPF), the National Data Protection Agency (ANPD) and the National Consumer Secretariat (Senacon) sent a recommendation to WhatsApp[154] to protect the rights of data subjects and the rights of consumers, in addition to mitigating potential effects on competition arising from the new policy to be implemented. This recommendation is very important not only regarding its effects on the protection of rights but, above all, it shows that these bodies are acting in a coordinated manner, which is essential to effectively guarantee privacy and freedom and, especially, to reduce informational asymmetry.

687. It is important to notice that the Criminal LGPD draft bill, if approved, would also perform an interesting role for law enforcement in Brazil. That is because it brings provisions related to the processing of personal data in cases of national defense, public security, investigation, and prosecution of criminal offenses.

688. Within its application scope, the draft bill establishes new forms of sanctioning public organs and entities that do not strictly follow its commands. In Article 52 of the draft bill, 3 possible sanctions are listed: warning with an indication of the deadline for adopting corrective measures; blocking the personal data to which the infraction refers until its regularization, when applicable; partial suspension of the operation of the database to which the infraction refers to, for a maximum period of two months, extendable for the same period, until the regularization of the processing activity by the controller, when applicable.

689. Alongside the noted provisions, the draft bill also relates to some conditions that may aggravate or mitigate the sanction, also determining that the extension of it shall be decided, taking into consideration the severity of the injury and the culpability of the agent.

154. Cade, MPF, ANPD e Senacon recomendam que WhatsApp adie entrada em vigor da nova política de privacidade—Português (Brasil) (www.gov.br).

690. This whole new enforcement system, if really turned into law, will not be superior to any previous legislation; instead, it shall be interpreted in line with the other national provisions and laws within the scope of data protection and information security in order to create a more specific and effective defense line for the data subjects in Brazil.

Chapter 3. National Security Services

691. The European framework of privacy and data protection encompasses, beyond the GDPR, Directive No. 680/2016, which is related to the protection of natural persons regarding the processing of personal data by competent authorities for the purposes of the prevention, investigation, detection or prosecution of criminal offenses or the execution of criminal penalties, and on the free movement of such data.[155]

692. This directive protects the fundamental right to data protection in situations where personal data is used by criminal law enforcement authorities, such as police and judicial authorities. It aims to ensure that the personal data of victims, witnesses and suspects of crimes are properly protected and to facilitate transnational cooperation in the fight against crime and terrorism.[156]

693. In the Brazilian legal system, the issues with privacy and data protection are not fully regulated. An example of this is the data protection applied to national security services. Accordingly, to Article 4, item III of the LGPD, the legislation does not apply to the processing of personal data that is done exclusively for purposes of public safety, national defense, state security or activities of investigation and prosecution of criminal offenses. However, there is legislation that indirectly protects the privacy and personal data:

§1. Interception of Telecommunications Act (Law No. 9.296/1996)

694. This legislation establishes requirements that must be complied with by the authority in situations of telephone calls interception. In accordance with Article 2 of the Law, the requirements like (i) reasonable signs of authorship or participation in a criminal offense, (ii) no other means available to constitute evidence, and (iii) the investigated fact constitutes a criminal offense punishable at most by detention must be applied in the case.

695. Furthermore, the determination of the interception must be a court order reasoned and with methods of execution of the diligence. The deadline for the interception is fifteen days renewable for an equal period once the indispensability of the means of proof is proven.[157]

155. European Union. Data protection in the EU. 2021. https://ec.europa.eu/info/law/law-topic/data-protection/data-protection-eu_pt.
156. *Ibid*.
157. http://www.planalto.gov.br/ccivil_03/leis/l9296.htm.

§2. Criminal Organization Act (Law No. 12.850/2013)

696. This Law provides for the possibility of access to personal information during the criminal prosecution phase in order to obtain evidence of authorship and materiality. In accordance with Article 3 are means of proof, the access to records of telephone and telematic communications, registration data contained in public or private data banks and electoral or commercial information, the interception of telephone and telematic communications, the removal of financial, banking and tax secrecy, pursuant to specific legislation, among others. It is important to mention that the means of proof must be a balance between the public interest and the privacy of the defendant.[158]

§3. Access to Information Act (Law No. 12.527/2011)

697. The access to information act guarantees that the restrictions to access personal data cannot harm criminal prosecution. According to Article 24, the information held by public organs and entities, observing its content and in view of its indispensability to the security of society or the State, may be classified as top secret, secret or reserved. Nonetheless, information considered essential to the security of society or of the State shall be liable to classification and restricted access in accordance with Article 23.[159]

698. Hence, as mentioned, there are many legislation that indirectly protect privacy and personal data. Finally, it must be mentioned that the first paragraph of Article 4 of LGPD establishes that the processing of personal data for public safety, national defense, state security or activities of investigation and prosecution of criminal offenses shall be governed by specific legislation, which shall provide proportional and strictly necessary measures for fulfilling the public interest, subject to due legal process, the general principles of protection and the rights of the data subjects as provided in this Law.

699. Therefore, due to the fact that the LGPD determines that another legislation must regulate the processing of personal data for national security matters, Brazilian parliamentarians have mobilized to develop a draft law on the subject at the end of 2019.[160] It is expected that this legislation will be drafted and enacted soon and will form part of the body of the Brazilian legal system regarding data protection.

158. http://www.planalto.gov.br/ccivil_03/_ato2011-2014/2013/lei/l12850.htm.
159. http://www.planalto.gov.br/ccivil_03/_ato2011-2014/2011/lei/l12527.htm.
160. https://www.camara.leg.br/noticias/618483-maia-cria-comissao-de-juristas-para-propor-lei-sobre-uso-de-dados-pessoais-em-investigacoes/.

Chapter 4. Implementing the Brazilian Data Protection Law as a Form to Reassure the Principle of Free Competition in a Surveillance Capitalism Era

700. Deeply analyzing the impacts brought by the Industrial Revolution 4.0, essentially having the processing of personal data as the main means, the Brazilian Data Protection Law, through the legality of adequacy imposed on various organizations, can serve as a means of reducing risks to violations the principle of free competition, guaranteeing the perpetuity of the Brazilian economic order.

701. The principle of free competition is constitutionally guaranteed, having been included with others (principles of the economic order), being an imposing constitutional principle, presented in two ways, as it produces the idea of formal legal equality even if it involves inequality at the end of the competition.[161]

702. The same principle was also embraced by the Brazilian Data Protection Law (Article 2, VI of Law 13.709/18), which within the scope of this new law, mainly brings a new right to the Brazilian law, the right to data protection as a fundamental right. However, dealing with the principle of free competition associated with the Brazilian Data Protection Law makes the purpose of the law extend to an understanding through a broader perspective, turning to the economic matter in view of the connection of the activity in which it is regulated by law (data processing for economic purposes—Article 3, item II from the Brazilian Data Protection Law) and current trade movements, in which they depend on an unusual asset when compared to other moments of change in the social, economic and industrial fabric.

703. This transition still experienced by the economic sphere is the result of a movement named by Klaus Schwab, president of the World Economic Forum (WEF), as the fourth Industrial Revolution.

704. We are witnessing profound shifts across all industries, marked by the emergence of new business models, the disruption of incumbents and the reshaping of production, consumption, transportation and delivery systems (Schwab, 2016, p. 7).

705. Of course, as presented by Schwab, many of these changes are still in their infancy, but they are already reaching an inflation point, even during their development, merging with technology through the physical, digital, and biological world and the economy.

706. And within the economic sphere, organizations have noticed the profit potential when using an asset that is highlighted in this new industrial milestone: personal data. This new matrix that drives this new business chain has been, however contradictory, for many years, being mined in various ways, implying a mode

161. Eros Roberto Grau, *A ordem econômica na constituição de 1988* 244 (Malheiros Editoras 6th ed.).

of production that differs from those commonly analyzed, but due to technological advances and widespread use from the internet, data has become increasingly easy to obtain.

707. The unwanted exposure of a person to the eyes of others happens more often today through the disclosure of their personal data than through the intrusion into their home, the dissemination of news about them in the press, the violation of their correspondence—in short, through the media formerly "classics" of privacy violations (Doneda, 2019, p. 11).

708. While even some nations have left archaic modes of production, the current panorama is turning to a new model based on surveillance. From the perspective of Marx in his "Contribution to the Critique of Political Economy," right in his preface, it is possible to identify some compositional characteristics of a mode of production, such as the correspondence of production relations (determined, necessary, independent of human will) at a specific level of development of its material productive forces, and which in its entirety constitute an economic mesh, under which there is a legal, political and ideological superstructure (Marx, 2008, p. 47). It is in this interim that surveillance capitalism takes place as a mode of production when analyzed through the concepts given by Zuboff:

> 1. A new economic order that claims human experience as free raw material for hidden commercial practices of extraction, prediction, and sales; 2. A parasitic economic logic in which the production of goods and services is subordinated to a new global architecture of behavioral modification; 3. A rogue mutation of capitalism marked by concentrations of wealth, knowledge, and power unprecedented in human history; 4. The foundational framework of a surveillance economy; 5. As significant a threat to human nature in the twenty-first century as industrial capitalism was to the natural world in the nineteenth and twentieth; 6. The origin of a new instrumentarian power that asserts dominance over society and presents startling challenges to market democracy; 7. A movement that aims to impose a new collective order based on total certainty; 8. An expropriation of critical human rights that is best understood as a coup from above: an overthrow of the people's sovereignty. (Zuboff, 2018, p. 8)

709. Its concepts fulfill the possible requirements named by Marx so that surveillance capitalism can be understood as a mode of production. Of course, the order does not cease to be capitalist, but the mode of production changes, given that the role played by other modes of production and their productive and material forces in society are in contradiction with the existing relations of production (Marx, 2008, p. 47).

710. When dealing with the existing production relationships in market 4.0, the premise that this project brings is that data processing becomes part of the whole of market 4.0. Initially, it should be understood that personal data (Article 5, items I and II/LGPD) are the raw material, which after being extracted and processed by the most diverse technologies, will be converted into information, as shown by the importance of this differentiation Sousa and da Silva:

> The data is related to a set of facts or description of distinct and objective events that, in its isolated or primary form, does not make any sense.
>
> [...]
>
> As for information, it can be said that it arises from data and can be understood as the meaning attributed to it, based on the context involved, on the user's need and on the subject's domain. In other words, the information constitutes the data interpreted in an analytical process in which its creation depends on the understanding and attribution of meaning to them (Sousa & Da Silva, 2020, p. 4).

711. Data as assets, along with advances in ICTs, become raw material for an economy in which the personal data of citizens will come to dictate the logic of capital accumulation for the generation of wealth (Bioni, 2020, p. 11) by the companies that own them. This key activity for the surveillance capitalist mode of production would be framed in what the Brazilian Data Protection Law determines as the processing of personal data (Article 5, X/LGPD), and in order to carry out the processing activities, organizations must then be aligned with their legal demands.

712. Virtual practices presuppose transparency, collaboration, knowledge sharing and the ability to mobilize the network. They also presuppose new attitudes and behaviors in social media, the growing development of digital citizenship, with waves of political mobilization and greater dialogue between individuals, government and companies (Araujo, 2017, p. 21).

713. There is a legal duty to comply with the law in view of the risks associated with noncompliance with what the LGPD says. It is due to the legality of adequacy demanded by the aforementioned data protection law that forms of mitigation of the risks imposed by the single domain of businesses arise that use such economic activity based on the surveillance capitalist mode of production.

714. For Ulrich Beck, the current condition of systems is that of being at risk, being a serial product of progress (Beck, 2010, p. 33), his analysis of this economic aspect also serves. In free market economies, the focal point turns to the freedom that economic and industrial activities have due to the existence of principles aimed at the exercise of economic activity as a fundamental vector of development (Neto, 2017, p. 57). It appears that there is no implicit desire of the state to nationalize economic relations, but capitalism depends on it, being preserved when the state is called upon to act in the economic domain (Grau, 2001, p. 28).

715. Within this context, as a mechanism to protect the Brazilian capitalist order, it is faced with the defense of free competition in the aforementioned devices: The constitution, Brazilian Data Protection Law and its own law (Law 12.529/11). It is through this principle that an efficient allocation of resources in the economy is allowed, lower prices and greater innovation, and that from the moment that production goods and services are in the domain of the monopolist, the established rights of the Brazilian economic order are infringed (Todorov & Torres Filho, 2014, p. 7). It is within Law 12.529/11 that we will find the protection of free competition, allowing those harmed by anti-competitive acts to be brought to justice, preventing unfair practices that are offensive to the economic order (*ibid.*, p. 47).

716. As in the Brazilian jurisdiction, the Gesetz gegen den unlauteren Wettbewerb, UWG (German Law Against Unfair Competition), seeks to protect competition, consumers and other market "players" against unfair commercial practices so as to maintain equity in the competitive games existing within from the market. Regarding this project, a specific case could serve as a comparison and support the debate through comparative law, being it between the German competition authority (Bundeskartellamt) against Facebook, which in a recent decision provisionally confirmed the allegation of abuse of position dominant by Facebook. The use of this real case, however, in another territory, could be used as a good role model for the 4.0 market in Brazil.

Bibliography

An Coimisiún um Chosaint Sonrái Data Protection Commission. Codes of Conduct. Available at: https://www.dataprotection.ie/en/organisations/codes-conduct. Accessed on: November 18, 2021.

An Coimisiún um Chosaint Sonrái Data Protection Commission. GDPR Certification. Available at: https://www.dataprotection.ie/en/organisations/gdpr-certificati on. Accessed on: November 18, 2021.

ANDP. Agente de Tratamento. Available at: https://www.gov.br/anpd/pt-br/canais_atendimento/agente-de-tratamento/transferencia-internacional-de-dados. Accessed December 20, 2021.

ANDP. ANPD assina Memorando de Entendimento com a Agência Espanhola de Proteção de Dados. Available at: https://www.gov.br/anpd/pt-br/assuntos/noticias /anpd-assina-memorando-de-entendimento-com-a-agencia-espanhola-de-proteca o-de-dados. Accessed on December 23 and 25, 2021.

ANDP. ANPD torna-se membro da Rede Ibero-Americana de proteção de dados. Available at: https://www.gov.br/anpd/pt-br/assuntos/noticias/anpd-torna-se-mem bro-da-rede-ibero-americana-de-protecao-de-dados. Accessed on December 26, 2021.

ANDP. Nota Técnica No. 37/2021/CGN/ANPD. Relatório de Acompanhamento e Execução da Agenda Regulatória para o biênio 2021–2022—2/2021. Available at: https://www.gov.br/anpd/pt-br/assuntos/sei_00261-000027_2021_64.pdf. Accessed on: December 20, 2021.

ANPD. Canais de Atendimento, Agente de Tratamento, Transferência Internacional de Dados. Available at: https://www.gov.br/anpd/pt-br/canais_atendimento/agent e-de-tratamento/transferencia-internacional-de-dados. Accessed on: November 28, 2021.

ANPD. Planejamento estratégico. Available at: https://www.gov.br/anpd/pt-br/docu mentos-e-publicacoes/planejamento-estrategico/planejamento-estrategico-2021-2 023.pdf. Accessed on December 20, 2021.

ANPD. Portaria n º 11, de 27 de janeiro de 2021. Torna pública a agenda regulatória para o biênio 2021-2022. Availabe at: https://www.in.gov.br/en/web/dou/ -/portaria-n-11-de-27-de-janeiro-de-2021-301143313. Accessed on: November 26, 2021

ANPD. Proposta de Cadeia de Valor e Macroprocessos da ANPD. Available at: htt ps://www.gov.br/anpd/pt-br/acesso-a-informacao/transparencia-e-prestacao-de-c ontas-1/transparencia-e-prestacao-de-contas-2021/cadeia_de_valor_anpd___final .pdf. Accessed on: December 20, 2021.

Bibliography

Araújo, A. "The Right to Data Protection and the Commissions' Adequacy Decision," *UNIO—EU Law Journal*, 1 (2015): 77–93. Available at: doi:10.21814/unio.1.6. Accessed on: November 21, 2021.

Autoridade Nacional de Proteção de Dados. Portaria No. 11, de 27 de janeiro de 2021, Torna pública a agenda regulatória para o biênio 2021–2022. Available at: https://www.in.gov.br/en/web/dou/-/portaria-n-11-de-27-de-janeiro-de-2021-301143313. Accessed on: November 15, 2021.

Autoridade Nacional de Proteção de Dados. Transferência internacional de dados. Available at: https://www.gov.br/anpd/pt-br/canais_atendimento/agente-de-tratamento/transferencia-internacional-de-dados. Accessed on: November 15, 2021.

Azambuja, Antonio João Gonçalves de, et al. "The Privacy, Security of the Information and Data Protection in Big Data." *Parc. The Strat. Brasília-DF*, 24(48) (January/June, 2019): 9–32, . Available at: http://seer.cgee.org.br/index.php/parcerias_estrategicas/article/viewFile/914/831. Accessed on: October 15, 2021.

Bastos, Athena. "Digital Law: Guide to the General Law on the Protection of Personal Data: The LGPD" (2018P. Available at: https://blog.sajadv.com.br/direito-digital-lei-de-protecaode-dados/. Accessed on: October 10, 2021.

Bioni, Bruno R. *Proteção de dados pessoais: a função e os limites do consentimento*. 2nd edition. Rio de Janeiro: Forense, 2019.

Bioni, Bruno R. & Laura M. Schertel. Regulamento Europeu de Proteção de Dados Pessoais e a Lei Geral brasileira de Proteção de Dados: mapeando convergências na direção de um nível de equivalência. 2019.

Bioni, Bruno Ricardo. *Proteção de Dados Pessoais—A Função e os Limites do Consentimento*. 3rd edição. Rio de Janeiro, Brazil: Grupo GEN, 2021. https://integrada.minhabiblioteca.com.br/books/9788530994105.

Bioni, B. Ricardo. From 2010 to 2018: The Brazilian Discussion on a General Law Data Protection. 2018a. Available at: https://brunobioni.com.br/blog/2018/07/02/de-2010-a-2018-a-discussao-brasileirasobre-uma-lei-geral-de-protecao-de-dados/. Accessed on: October 10, 2021.

Brasil. Constituição da República Federativa do Brasil de 1988. Available at: http://planalto.gov.br/ccivil_03/constituicao/constituicao.htm. Accessed on: November 20, 2021.

Brasil, Lei No. 12.965, Marco Civil da Internet. 2014. Available at: http://www.planalto.gov.br/ccivil_03/_ato2011-2014/2014/lei/l12965.htm. Access on: November 20, 2021.

Brasil. Lei Geral De Proteção De Dados Pessoais. Lei no 13.709, de 14 de agosto de 2018. Available at: http://www.planalto.gov.br/ccivil_03/_ato2015-2018/2018/lei/l13709.htm. Accessed on: November 21, 2021.

Brazil. Brazilian Civil Code. Law No. 10. 406, January 10, 2002. 2002. Articles 1, 2 and 3.

Brazil. Brazilian Data Protection Law (LGPD). Law No. 18.709, August 14, 2018. 2018.

Brazil. Brazilian Data Protection Law (LGPD). Law No. 18.709, August 14, 2018. 2018.

Brazil. Brazilian Data Protection Law (LGPD). Law No. 18.709, August 14, 2018. 2018.

Brazil. Brazilian Data Protection Law (LGPD). Law No. 18.709, August 14, 2018. 2018.

Brazil. Brazilian Data Protection Law (LGPD). Law No. 18.709, August 14, 2018. 2018.

Brazil. Consumer's Right Act. Law No. 8.708, September 11, 1990. 1990.

Brazil. Consumer's Right Act. Law No. 8.708, September 11, 1990. 1990.

Brazil. Decree-Law n. 2.848, December 7, 1940. Criminal Code. Official Journal of the Union, Rio de Janeiro, December. 31, 1940.

Brazil. Federal Supreme Court. STF concludes that right to be forgotten is incompatible with the Federal Constitution. 2021. https://portal.stf.jus.br/noticias/verNoticiaDetalhe.asp?idConteudo=460414&ori=1.

Brazil. House of Representatives. 2021. https://www.camara.leg.br/noticias/618483-maia-cria-comissao-de-juristas-para-propor-lei-sobre-uso-de-dados-pessoais-em-investigacoes/.

Brazil. Law 13.709 of August 14, 2018. 2018.

Brazil. Law No. 10.406, January 10, 2002. Establishes the Civil Code. Official Journal of the Union: Section 1, Brasília, DF, year 139, n. 8, 1–74, January 11, 2002.

Brazil. Law No. 12.527, of November 18, 2011. http://www.planalto.gov.br/ccivil_03/_ato2011-2014/2011/lei/l12527.htm.

Brazil. Law No. 12.850, of August 2, 2013. http://www.planalto.gov.br/ccivil_03/_ato2011-2014/2013/lei/l12850.htm.

Brazil. Law No. 9.296, of July 24, 1996. http://www.planalto.gov.br/ccivil_03/leis/l9296.htm.

Brazil. Law No. 10,406 of January 10, 2002. Civil code. Official Gazette of União, Brasilia, January 10, 2002. Available at: http://http://www.planalto.gov.br/ccivil_03/leis/2002/l10406.htm/. Accessed: October 15, 2021.

Brazil. Law No. 13,709 of August 14, 2018. General data protection law. Official Gazette, Brasilia, August 14, 2018. Available at: http://www.planalto.gov.br/ccivil_03/_ato2015-2018/2018/lei/L13709.htm/. Access in: October 5, 2021.

Brazil. Second Version. Guidelines for Definitions of Agents of Processing of Personal Data and of the DPO. April 2022.

Brazilian Competition Law. Law No. 12.529/2011. http://www.planalto.gov.br/ccivil_03/_ato2011-2014/2011/lei/l12529.htm.

Brazilian Data Protection Law. Law No. 13.70/2018. http://www.planalto.gov.br/ccivil_03/_ato2015-2018/2018/lei/L13709.htm.

Brazilian Data Protection Law. Law 13.709. 2018. BRA. Available at: http://www.planalto.gov.br/ccivil_03/_ato2015-2018/2018/lei/L13709.htm/. Accessed on: November 17, 2021.

Cade, MPF, ANPD e Senacon recomendam que WhatsApp adie entrada em vigor da nova política de privacidade. Federal Government, Brasília, May 7, 2021. Available at https://www.gov.br/anpd/pt-br/assuntos/noticias/cade-mpf-anpd-e-senacon-recomendam-que-whatsapp-adie-entrada-em-vigor-da-nova-politica-de-privacidade#:~:text=O%20Conselho%20Administrativo%20de%20Defesa,pol%C3%ADtica%20de%20privacidade%20do%20aplicativo. Accessed on: December 2.

Cathy, O'Neil. Available at: https://hdsr.mitpress.mit.edu/pub/j8y5fwco/release/1. Accessed on: November 17, 2021.

Bibliography

Chang, Alvin. *The Facebook and Cambridge Analytica Scandal Explained with a Simple Diagram*. Vox, 2018. Available at: https://www.vox.com/policy-and-politics/2018/3/23/17151916/facebook-cambridge-analytica-trump-diagram. Accessed on: November 21, 2021.

Consolidation of Labor Laws. Law No. 5453. 1943. Available at: http://www.planalto.gov.br/ccivil_03/decreto-lei/del5452.htm. Accessed on: November 17, 2021.

Constitution of the Federative Republic of Brazil: Constitutional Text Enacted on October 5, 1988, with the Alterations Established by Revision Constitutional Amendments No. 1, 1994 Through 6, 1994, by Constitutional Amendments No. 1, 1992 Through 92, 2016, and by Legislative Decree No. 186, 2008.—5th. edition.—Brasília: Chamber of Deputies, Edições Câmara, 2016.—(Série textos básicos; n. 132 PDF).

Constitution of the Federative Republic of Brazil: Constitutional text of October 5, 1988, with the alterations introduced by Constitutional Amendments Nos. 1/92 through 72/2013 and by Revision Constitutional Amendments Nos. 1/94 through 6/94.

Court of Labor Court of the 4th Region. Civil Public Civil Action 0020014-30.2021.5.04.0261. July 13, 2021.

Doneda, Danilo. 2020. Da privacidade à proteção de dados pessoais: elementos da formação da Lei Geral de Proteção de Dados. 2nd edition. São Paulo, Brazil. Thomson Reuters Brasil.

Doneda, Danilo. Da Privacidade à Proteção de Dados Pessoais. 2nd edition. São Paulo: Thomson Reuters Brasil, 2020.

EDPB. Guidelines 1/2019 on Codes of Conduct and Monitoring Bodies under Regulation 2016/679. Available at: https://edpb.europa.eu/sites/default/files/files/file1/edpb_guidelines_201901_v2.0_codesofconduct_en.pdf. Accessed on: December 1, 2021.

EU General Data Protection Regulation (GDPR): Regulation (EU) 2016/679 of the European Parliament and of the Council of 27 April 2016 on the protection of natural persons with regard to the processing of personal data and on the free movement of such data, and repealing Directive 95/46/EC (General Data Protection Regulation), OJ 2016 L 119/1.

EU General Data Protection Regulation (GDPR): Regulation (EU) 2016/679 of the European Parliament and of the Council of 27 April 2016 on the protection of natural persons with regard to the processing of personal data and on the free movement of such data, and repealing Directive 95/46/EC (General Data Protection Regulation), OJ 2016 L 119/1.

European Data Protection Board. Guidelines 1/2019 on Codes of Conduct and Monitoring Bodies under Regulation 2016/679. Available at: https://edpb.europa.eu/sites/default/files/files/file1/edpb_guidelines_201901_v2.0_codesofconduct_en.pdf Accessed on: November 22, 2021.

European Data Protection Board. Guidelines 4/2018 on the accreditation of certification bodies under Article 43 of the General Data Protection Regulation (2016/679). Available at: https://edpb.europa.eu/sites/default/files/files/file1/edpb_guidelines_201804_v3.0_accreditationcertificationbodies_annex1_en.pdf. Accessed on: November 22, 2021.

European Union. Data protection in the EU. 2021. https://ec.europa.eu/info/law/law-topic/data-protection/data-protection-eu_pt.

FGV. Guia de Proteção de Dados Pessoais—Transferência Internacional Versão 1.0—Outubro, 2020, 1–34.

Filho, C.S. Direito Concorrencial. 1st edition. São Paulo, Brasil. Malheiros, January 2021.

Flesch, Jose Norberto. Brasil começa modelo de remessa de dados com clausula padrão, diz ANPD. Available at: https://www.telesintese.com.br/brasil-comeca-modelo-de-remessa-de-dados-com-clausula-padrao-diz-anpd/ Accessed on: November 26, 2021.

Frazão, Ana. Lei Geral de Proteção de Dados e suas Repercussões no Direito Brasileiro. 1st edition. São Paulo: Thomson Reuters Brasil, 2019.

Garcia, L.R. Lei Geral de Proteção de Dados (LGPD): Guia de implantação. São Paulo: Editora Blucher, 2020.

General Court. Document 62017CJ0040. Available on: https://eur-lex.europa.eu/legal-content/EN/TXT/?uri=CELEX%3A62017CJ0040. Accessed on: November 7, 2022.

Germany. Federal Constitutional Court. 2021. https://www.bundesverfassungsgericht.de/SharedDocs/Entscheidungen/EN/1983/12/rs19831215_1bvr020983en.html.

Goldberg, Samuel G., Garrett A. Johnson & Scott K. Shriver. *Regulating Privacy Online: An Economic Evaluation of the GDPR*. Marketing Science Institute Working Paper Series, Report No. 21-110, 2021.

Grau, E.R. A ordem econômica na constituição de 1988. São Paulo, Brazil. Malheiros Editoras, 2001.

Hintzbergen, Jule, et al. Fundamentos Segurança da Informação. 3rd edition. São Paulo: Brasport 2018.

IAPP. Data Protection Authority. 2020.

ICO. Guide to the General Data Protection Regulation (GDPR), Accountability and Governance, Certification. Available at: https://ico.org.uk/for-organisations/guide-to-data-protection/guide-to-the-general-data-protection-regulation-gdpr/accountability-and-governance/certification/. Accessed on: December 1, 2021.

ICO. Guide to the General Data Protection Regulation (GDPR): Codes of Conduct. Available at: https://ico.org.uk/for-organisations/guide-to-data-protection/guide-to-the-general-data-protection-regulation-gdpr/accountability-and-governance/codes-of-conduct/. Accessed on: December 1, 2021.

Information Commission Officer. Codes of Conduct. What Are Codes of Conduct?. Available at: https://ico.org.uk/for-organisations/guide-to-data-protection/guide-to-the-general-data-protection-regulation-gdpr/accountability-and-governance/codes-of-conduct/. Accessed on: November 20, 2021.

Jusbrasil. Vieira, Victor. LGDP Transferencia internacional de dados. Available at: https://vieiravictor.jusbrasil.com.br/artigos/726523659/lei-geral-de-protecao-de-dados-transferencia-internacional-de-dados-pessoais. Accessed on December 26, 2021.

Kuner, Christopher. "Reality and Illusion in EU Data Transfer Regulation Post Schrems (July 7, 2017)." German Law Journal 18 (2017): 881. Available at: https://ssrn.com/abstract=2732346 or http://dx.doi.org/10.2139/ssrn.2732346. Accessed on: December 1, 2021.

Bibliography

Marx, K. Contribuição à Crítica da Economia Política. 2nd edition. São Paulo, Brasil. Editora Expressão Popular, 2008.

Mendes, Laura Schertel. Privacidade, proteção de dados e defesa do consumidor. 1st edition. Editora Saraiva, 2014.

National Personal Data Protection Authority. National Authority for the Protection of Personal Data (ANPD) Completes 1 year. 2021.

National System of Minestries. Law No. 10.826. 2003. BRA. Available at: http://www.planalto.gov.br/ccivil_03/leis/2003/l10.826.htm. Accessed on: November 17, 2021.

O'Neil, Cathy. Weapons of Math Destruction: How Big Data Increases Inequality and Threatens Democracy. Crown Publishing Group (NY), 2016. Available at: https://edisciplinas.usp.br/pluginfile.php/5971949/mod_resource/content/1/%28FFLCH%29%20LIVRO%20Weapons%20of%20Math%20Destruction%20-%20Cathy%20ONeal.pdf.. Accessed on: November 17, 2021.

Pinheiro, Patricia Peck. Proteção de Dados Pessoais. 3rd dição). São Paulo. SaraivaJur, 2021.

Pinheiro, Patricia Peck. *Personal Data Protection: Comments on Law n. 13.709/2018*. 3rd edn. São Paulo: Editora SaraivaJur, 2021.

Pinheiro, Patricia Peck. Proteção de dados pessoais. Comentários à Lei n. 13.709/2018 (LGPD). 23ª Edição. Saraiva, Capítulo V, 2020.

Portal STF. Brazil. STF conclui que direito ao esquecimento é incompatível com a Constituição Federal. Available at https://portal.stf.jus.br/noticias/verNoticiaDetalhe.asp?idConteudo=460414&ori=1. Accessed on: December 6, 2021.

Regulation (EU) 2016/679 of the European Parliament and of the Council of 27 April 2016 on the protection of natural persons with regard to the processing of personal data and on the free movement of such data and repealing Directive 95/46/EC (General Data Protection Regulation), OJ 2016 L 119/1.

Rennó Penteado Sampaio Advogados. Translation by Ronaldo Lemos, Natalia Langenegger, Juliana Pacetta Ruiz, Sofia Lima Franco, Andréa Guimarães Gobbato, Daniel Douek, Ramon Alberto dos Santos and Rafael A. Ferreira Zanatta. As amended by Law No. 13,583, after congressional override of presidential vetoes. This translation was based on an initial version by Monica Hruby (www.mhruby.com). Available at: https://iapp.org/media/pdf/resource_center/Brazilian_General_Data_Protection_Law.pdf. Accessed on: December 21, 2021.

Sander, William. Main Concepts of the LGPD. 2019. Available at: https://sisqualis.com.br/conceitos-lgpd/. Accessed on: October 5, 2021.

Schwab, Klaus. *The Fourth Industrial Revolution*. Cologny/Geneva: World Economic Forum, 2016.

Schwabe, Jürgen. *50 Years of Case-Law of the German Federal Constitutional Court*. Translate: Beatriz Hennig et al. Montevidéu: Fundacion Konrad-Adenauer, 2005. Available at: http://www.kas.de/wf/doc/kas_7738-544-1- 30.pdf. Accessed on: April 11, 2020, 237.

Sombra, Thiago Luís Santos. Fundamentos da regulação da privacidade e proteção de dados pessoais: pluralismo jurídico e transparência em perspectiva. São Paulo: Thomson Reuters Brasil, 2019.

Souza, C.A., M. Viola & R. Lemos. *Brazil's Internet Bill of Rights: A Closer Look*. 2nd edn. Rio de Janeiro: ITS Rio, 2018.

STJ, REsp 1,348,532—SP, Min. Rel. Luís Felipe Salomão, 4th T, DJ: October 10, 2017.

SwissCam. LGPD: authorization for international transfer and regulation by ANPD. Renata Armonia, Bruno Guilhem e Natália Dantas Fleury, Coimbra & Rhomberg Advogados. Available at: https://swisscam.com.br/en/publicacao/doing-business-in-brazil/33-brazilian-general-data-protection-law-lgpd/. Accessed on December 22, 2021.

Teffé, C.S. de & M. Viola. Tratamento de dados pessoais na LGPD: estudo sobre as bases legais, civilistica.com, 9(1), 1–38. Available at: https://civilistica.emnuvens.com.br/redc/article/view/510. Accessed on: January 21, 2022.

Telesintese. Brasil começa modelo de remessa de dados com cláusula padrão, diz anpd. Available at: https://www.telesintese.com.br/brasil-comeca-modelo-de-remessa-de-dados-com-clausula-padrao-diz-anpd/. Accessed on December 20, 2021.

TJPR, 0002916-31.2014.8.16.0184/0, Mag. Report. Renata Ribeiro Bau, 3rd TR, Dj: October 15, 2015.

Todorov, F.R. & M.M.T. Filho. Direito do Consumidor e Direito da Concorrência. Brazil. Secretaria de Acompanhamento Econômico, December 2014.

UN General Assembly. *Universal Declaration of Human Rights*, December 10, 1948, 217 A (III), https://www.refworld.org/docid/3ae6b3712c.html. Accessed on: October 3, 2021).

UN General Assembly, Universal Declaration of Human Rights, December 10, 1948, 217 A (III). Available at: https://www.refworld.org/docid/3ae6b3712c.html. Access on: November 17, 2021.

Ustaran, Eduardo. *European Data Protection Law and Practice*. Rochester Ave., Portsmouth: International Association of Privacy Professionals, 2018, 504.

Vasconcelos, Beto & Felipe De Paula. *Lei Geral de Proteção de Dados e suas Repercussões no Direito Brasileiro*. 1st edition. São Paulo: Thomson Reuters Brasil, 2019.

Ventura, Leonardo Henrique de Carvalho. Considerações sobre a nova lei geral de proteção de dados. Revista Síntese: Direito Administrativo, São Paulo, v. 13, n. 155, 56/64, 2018.

Viola, Mario. Transferência de Dados entre Europa e Brasil: Análise da Adequação da Legislação Brasileira. ITS. Rio de Janeiro. November 2019, 1–22.

Viola, Mario, Leonardo Heringer & Celina Carvalho. Relatorio-Transferencia-de-dados-pessoais.pdf. ITS Instituto de Tecnologia & Sociedade do Rio. Agosto 2021, 1–28.

Viola, Mario & Patrícia Thomazelli. Portabilidade de Dados, Interoperabilidade e Open Banking. ITS-Rio, 2021. Available at: https://itsrio.org/wp-content/uploads/2021/02/Portabilidade-Interoperabilidade-OpenBanking.pdf. Accessed on: December 2, 2022.

Warren, Samuel D. & Louis D. Brandeis. "The Right to Privacy." *Harvard Law Review*, 4(5) (1890): 193–220. JSTOR. Available at: www.jstor.org/stable/1321160. Accessed on: November 17, 2021.

Zuboff, Shoshana. The Age of Surveillance Capitalism: The Fight for a Human Future at the New Frontier of Power. 1st edn. New York: Public Affairs, January 2019.

Index

The numbers refer to paragraph numbers

Index

www.ingramcontent.com/pod-product-compliance
Lightning Source LLC
Chambersburg PA
CBHW071444230926
51846CB00001B/336

9789403535265